PAPER ARCHITECTURE
An exhibition of Deutsche Lufthansa AG., German Airlines

This exhibition has been organized by Deutsche Lufthansa AG
in cooperation with the Soviet Association of
Architects and has been generously sponsored
by Deutsche Lufthansa AG.

Deutsches Architektur Museum, Frankfurt am Main, 1989

US Tour 1990/1991

Massachusetts Institute of Technology, Cambridge, MA

The American Institute of Architects, Washington, D.C.

Yale University School of Architecture, New Haven, CT

Grey Art Gallery, New York University, New York City

Rice University School of Architecture, Houston, TX

PAPER ARCHITECTURE
NEW PROJECTS FROM THE SOVIET UNION

Edited by Heinrich Klotz

With an essay by
Alexander G. Rappaport

RIZZOLI
NEW YORK

Conception and selection by
Heinrich Klotz, Yuri Awwakumow and Michail Belov

Catalogue: Andrea Gleininger
Photographs: Igor Palmin
Cover: Victor B. Kornis
Translation: Christiane Court

First published in the United States of America in 1990
by Rizzoli International Publication, Inc.
300 Park Avenue South, New York, NY 10010

© 1988 Deutsches Architektur Museum, Frankfurt am Main
and Oktogon Verlag, Stuttgart and München

Typeset: M. Lohmaier, Rosenheim
Printed and bound in Jugoslavia by Gorenjski Tisk, Kranj
ISBN 0-8478-1284-7

Contents

Heinrich Klotz

Preface

Our first impressions of young Russian architects' projects in Moscow last year led us to believe that *glasnost* and *perestroika* were beginning to alter the building activity in the Soviet Union and that a new spirit of exploration was reflected in these projects. So we began to speak of a *perestroika* architecture, a notion, however, which our hosts emphatically rejected; they insisted that their concepts had been shaped by the Breshnev era. We pointed out that it was under Breshnev's rule that all those rigid, large buildings that have disfigured Moscow's image were erected − those huge fortifications of state-owned enterprises, that have even surpassed the Western disaster of "glass-box architecture". In response, we received a quick concessionary nod: it had been precisely this Breshnev-eraarchitecture, with its stagnation and lack of fantasy that caused them to rebel against the petrification and to mobilize counterforces on paper. Their "paper architecture" was not the result of a stimulus arising from the new situation, but a protest against a corrupted state architecture of former years. In that regard, their projects on paper had anticipated *glasnost* and *perestroika* and we meant to announce in the inner realm of fantasy what did not stand a chance in the outer realm of reality. They had become "paper architects" and had made that into a badge of honor.

Prevented from building and attacked by the established party architects, suspected of being reactionary and under pressure of not being able to act, they withdrew into their little offices − sketched, and invented stories. It was here, in shabby basement rooms, that we encountered a cornucopia of sketches, plans, large format presentation boards and models. Among these were many an unrealistic and daring project, many a drawing that its rebellion had slipped beyond control − but the impression of unexpected freshness and originality prevailed. The sharp contrast between the official architecture and these "paper castles" urged us to abandon the usual attitude of a certain condescension with which we normally react to the large scale state architecture of the Soviet Union. It was obvious that the young architects of the USSR were confronted with an interwoven, entangled ideological phalanx: with a politically rigid state and a concomitantly rigid architecture whose liaison was confirmed daily by an entrenched body of party architects.

Under these circumstances a neo-constructivist design in the style of Chernikov or Leonidov, or even colorful facade of a neo-Palladian villa, which in western eyes already seems obsolete in the sense of Postmodern, stereotyped historicism, presents itself as an act of liberation. The new shrine for the young Moscow architects is the restaurant of a private cooperative where beneath capitals and lions' head one can dine − well. This interior molded out of plaster of Paris,

7

dominated by four useless columns, freely placed in space, and idyllic to the point of kitsch with a babbling fountain, also awakens in us the delight of lapsing into mercly pleasurable and non-con-

frontational comfort. In the West, our critics, blessed with a more acute architectural discrimination, would most likely apply a karate chop to the fountain lion's mane - and that would be that! Here, however, the height of the columns can be experienced as the hardly-considered-possible redemption of secretly entertained wishes, as a daring protest against everything that, out there in the light of day, is prescribed by political and economic reason. Ornamentation and decoration have always been the rebellious, luxurious element that stood in the way of rational puritanism, punished by the slap of common sense and chased to hell with a hundred moral commandments. Here everything is reversed and the taw-

dry embellishment turns into the justification for survival. The valve opens under this pressure and hisses down to the level of a softer calmness. This, too, is *perestroika*.

The architectural projects of the Soviet architects depicted here are utopian. They are architectural picture stories dealing with buildings as if it could turn into a fabricated landscape of make-believe. The architecture becomes an allegory, a narrated event, sometimes a drama or a poem - in any event nothing static or firm. The esthetic character of architecture as fictitious coherence and invented order of events is emphasized. Often the drawings are accompanied by an explanatory text for transforming a proposed building into action. Architecture maintains the furthest imaginable distance from the merely functional; as a narration it invades the illusionary realm of esthetics, and rejects the identity of art and life to the point of pure fantasy. The revolt against an architecture of functionalism ignores any claim toward realization and reverts to the dream image, the brainchild. This is all beyond facts. As protest and melancholy retreat, as courageous abandonment of social injunctions and as a fictitious resistance, the drawings become exercises in survival of the imagination. The paper architects are not bound to stylistic injunctions. They speak the *lingua moderna* just as they submerge into Postmodern historicism. Their frame of reference is both the Soviet constructivism of the twenties as well as Palladio, Piranesi, Schinkel and Loos. The tempering through the Breshnev era has not deterred them from being pluralistic, like their Western colleagues; now, in Gorbachev's time, more so than ever. Whoever believed that the isolation of a political system could enforce uniformity of expression experiences just the opposite: the Soviet scene of paper architecture is no less pluralistic than that of Western democracies. European, American and Japanese architectural journals had been accessible for some time and could be read by students in the schools of architecture. There has not been complete isolation for years.

But for receptivity to develop, there had to be the motivation and drive: the willingness of the imagination to protest, which leads out of the pressure of being regulated.

We would like to express our heartfelt thanks for the friendly cooperation of our colleagues in Moscow, Yuri Awwakumov, Mikhail Belov and the vice-president of the Soviet architects' association Viatcheslav Glasitchev.

Heinz Ruhnau, chairman of the board of Deutsche Lufthansa, and his assistant, Nicolas Iljine, have given us exceptional support in initiating contacts with the Moscow architects. We owe special thanks to their personal commitment.

Heinrich Klotz
Deutsches Architekturmuseum

Alexander G. Rappaport

Language and Architecture of Post-Totalitarianism

The boom of "paper architeture" seems to be drawing to an end. In the Soviet Union, it had started when the young generation, in light of the Japanese idea-contests proved capable of what the older generation had long since given up: to win first prizes in established international architectural competitions. The young architects' success evoked surprise, enthusiasm and excitement among their own countrymen.

The first unrestricted showing of the masterpieces of paper architecture took place in literary surroundings, in the editorial office of the magazine "Junost" ("Youth"), which coincidentally is located opposite the project office of the city of Moscow (MOSPROJEKT). During the discussion concerning the individual projects, the enigmatic component of the phenomenon of paper architecture manifested itself. The young architects (primarily M. Belov) emphasized against protest of the older colleagues (although there was the former architect and now famous poet A. Vosnesenskij among them, who fully supported the participants), that they did not regard paper architecture as a surrogate of real architecture but as self-sufficient unto itself. In the press, reproaches were voiced that paper architecture withdrew from reality, from the urgent tasks of the national building program, and they were accused of individualism and a lack of seriousness. There were also, however, well-known defenders, who comprehended that the acuteness and graphic skill of the conceptualists were stronger than envy, that international recognition was advantageous for the State and that initiative should not be suppressed. They even made an effort to organize competitions themselves, although, here a paucity of means stood in the way of renown.

During the first attempts at a critical evaluation, above all emerged the variety of projects behind which, however, certain things in common could be sensed: the tendency to play with space, with cultural symbols, styles and with language, especially with the language of classicism (M. Fillippov and N. Bronsova) and of constuctivism (J. Awwakumov and others). The similarity between the experimental projects of I. Fomin and El Lissitzky leads one to think that this paper architecture represents a successor to the architecture of the twenties, when most projects remained on paper as well. One could be reminded of the project of the Palace of Soviets in 1930, which by a stroke of fate was turned in to an event in the world of paper architecture.

The group NER, however, which was founded in the mid-sixties and whose projects were not meant to be built but for theoretical examination only, has to be considered as the immediate predecessor for paper architecture. The leaders of the group, A. Gutnov and I. Leshava, who were teaching at the Moscow school of architecture, were directly or indirectly the teachers of many paper architects.

There are, however, also significant differences between the projects of the NER group and the conceptual projects of the eighties. Aside from the sharp contrast between the NER group and the routine of the bureaucratic city planning, both were based upon the same utopian models, from which the typical standard projects, service systems, the satellite towns and the industrial standardization of the sixties developed. This conformity of the NER group is most easily explicable through "stagnation" and bureaucratic control; at the same time in the West, however, the group "Archigram" was active who also was more receptive to modernity than the Postmodernists of the eighties.

Paper architecture can safely be regarded as an import of Postmodernism. This statement can be supported by the genre of paper architecture itself, as well as by the character of its graphics and the tendency towards the ironical inclusion of historical architectural styles, primarily classicism and constructivism; there is no need to explicitly emphasize the playful liberty that is typical for both Postmodernism and paper architecture.

To this very day the sense of this liberty has not been clearly understood. In part it either means liberation from the bureaucratic routine of the huge organizations whose work lies in the development of prototypical projects, the solution of production-line tasks as well as the consideration of industrial methods or the work on significant "representative" buildings. In part it is also a liberation from the principles of a sorberly functionalist architecture and the striving for a departure from the everyday limitations of life; a liberation which is not compatible with the bureaucratic cycle.

I think the specifics of the Soviet conceptual architecture of the eighties lie simultaneously in a postmodern rejection of the principles of modernity and, to an even greater degree, in the effort to withdraw from the protective cover of official architecture. This rejection had its origin in the totalitarian realization of certain principles of modern architecture, in an hitherto unattained standard of uniformity and subjection to the state. The nature of totalitarian architecture lies not only in gigantism or in the cult of power but also in a normative monotony which evolves in the course of a systematic realization of utopias. This clearly demonstrates the negative dialectics of freedom. The utopian schemes, that initially had evolved through creative activity were eventually confirmed as the ubiquituously valid norm of an authoritarian power, which in turn denies citizens the freedom to choose their architecture, and those architects who want to realize their own ideas, the freedom of activity.

The thought of realizing the utopia of a totally planned environment originated as early as the 18th century, but it was only in the 20th century that the technical and political conditions for such realization were created. Up to the 1980s it not only developed its own style (there had been several) and its own methodology (that of socialist realism), it was also disappointed by both, although this is a risky public statement to make even today. In the sixties totalitarian architecture could only be viewed from the aspect of an "improvement" − the NER group acted accordingly. In the eighties the young generation succeeded in withdrawing from the totalitarian bureaucratic control. Now the time has come to think about the future.

One cannot subsist on Japanese competitions. It is absolutely necessary to adjust to the reality of the national practice. Today the practice itself is ready for adjustment by offering a series of alternate forms for proposing, for example, the project cooperatives. As of now, however, there can be no unequivocal answer to the question whether the paper architects are capable of transforming the style and the genre of the conceptual competitions to practice. For this it is necessary to examine the peculiarities of paper architecture and its relation to the theory and practice of socialist architecture as it has taken shape during the decades of totalitarian culture.

To grasp the character of paper architecture, one must make a distinction between utopia and fantasy. The utopian thinking that had developed in the theory and practice of 19th and 20th century European architecture and in the architecture of the USSR denies pluralism.

A utopian project is based on a univeral perception of space which results in a general possibility of realization; the specific spatial conditions (geographical as well as human) may in fact influence the project but cannot fundamentally change it.

Fantasy resembles utopia in many respects but it is more comprehensive. Fantasy also encompasses a possible vision of the world, although, unlike utopia, fantasy does not really claim this vision to be the key to the solution of urgent human problems. Fantasy proceeds from the principle of a pluralistic world and the variety of the spatial conditions of human life. The spatiality of concrete fantasy is limited. It can be valid for a dictated as well as for an agreed upon location. The theatricality of fantasy is obvious; it emphasizes its relativity, the frame and the ramp. Utopia strives to abolish this relativity; not only does it destroy the spatial limits, but it also places the esthetics observer in the position of a participant until his mask corresponds to his face.

The differences between utopia and fantasy relating to time categories are analogous. The time of utopia is either "eternity", an era of the past (the "Golden Age") or of the future ("the happy future") which does not possess logical reversibility. Fantasy is, in large measure arbitrary; it can appear and disappear. Fantasy is subject to human will, while utopia on the other hand forces humans under its will and often also under its arbitrariness. Utopia has an imperative nature; on the one hand it impresses the controlling power, while on the other hand it incorporates in itself utopian features: the unity of totalitarian power corresponds to the unity of the author's will and derives from their combination the fictitious unity as well as the real uniformity.

The above does not exhaust the typological differentiations between utopia and fantasy; it suffices, however, for the distinction between the "paper architecture" of the eignties and the utopia of the early 20th century; that is such classicist utopias as Fomin's and Sholtovskij's, such functionalist utopias as Le Corbusier's, Wright's, as well as the Soviet constructivists. The realizations of western utopias remained isolated cases of chaotic and pluralistic cities, whereas the Soviet projects were gradually incorporated into the practice of city planning and thus created a non-pluralistic monotony or a hierarchical environment which in turn influenced a whole generation of architects.

Among the utopian and totalitarian characteristics of Soviet architecture which were employed for a certain period belong the unity of style, the systematic distribution of the available building sites to individual public authorities, and the complete dependency on the institutionalized city-planning bureaucracy which always strove to promote the uniformity of the environment through a reduction of building technologies.

In a totalitarian society, norms that had been developed and introduced by state-run institutions took the place of individual needs. All this precludes the possibility of individual proposals and impedes any change in the practice of architecture.

In the totalitarian society, utopia becomes reality and thus makes every other reality seem like pluralistic arbitrariness which is in contradiction to the system to which the honorary title of "Socialist Realism" was awarded. The recent efforts to change this system are accompanied by attempts to expand beyond this scope. One can recognize the first beginnings of escape from this system, which the system itself wants to interpret as signs of reform. This is why we ought to return to the question of the interrelation between "Post-Totalitarianism" and Postmodernism. Postmodernism is not only to be seen as a rejection of totalitarian pretentions and unreflected symbolic foundations of modernity but also as an encompassing of the further development of its principles, especially a differentiation of its architectural characteristics. The question that arises concerning "Posttotalitarianism", whether it follows in the footsteps of the totalitarian culture it denies, remains open. Sometimes such an imitation can be seen in the indifference towards reality which remains untouched by the author's fantasy, thus becoming a reality in itself, and which is so typical for romanticism. If this reality is altered (or "reeducated") in a totalitarian culture it can simply be ignored in a post-totalitarian culture. The plurality of ideas is capable of changing the monism of state-directed concepts without, however, affecting either the real plurality or the existing world which remains outside of artistic or professional interests.

Paper architecture, of course, is only one part of the non-conformist culture which is only gradually acquiring its own right to exist in the USSR. The impending revision of the principles of socialist realism is turning out to be one of the common problems in all areas of artistic activity. It cannot be precluded however that their specific peculiarities might not leave much of the common ground remaining. Postmodernism is dissociating itself from the totalitarian demands of modernity in architecture.

For totality as an unrenouncable component of utopia turns into totalitarianism, becomes the result of an enforced realization of the total utopian pattern on the pluralistic material of human life and its natural environment.

The authoritarian power that guarantees this realization of totalitarian projects leaves behind a certain distrust of the process of realization that also exudes from the circle of paper archtitects. This, of course, represents an extreme, since the local realization of a private project does not lead to totality. The realization of a fantasy, however, far removed from real life, continues to maintain a totalitarian tinge.

On the other hand it is necessary for fantasy to find its realization in a totally different way from traditional architecture and utopia. It does not primarily concern the creation of buildings nor only the practice of social standardization and organization, but rather the materialization of the author's creative ideas in these projects as well as the propagation of their conclusions through exhibitions and publications.

By the transformation of the project into a graphic and partially literary work of art it seems as if the authors intended to emphasize the new meaning of these projects so that they become an independent cultural phenomenon. In a way Victor Hugo's prophecy is repeated and augmented in the 20th century by Marshall McLuhan: In the age of mass culture architecture can be pushed aside by literature or television. The "literary quality" of paper archtiecture is organically linked to its fantasy. The legends and explanations for many projects can be regarded as little narrations or poems. This peculiarity of the conceptual projects is referred to by K. Beum as the "narrative" element. The attempt to find an explanation for this phenomenon, which emerges unexpectedly in architecture, leads us in two directions. On the one hand the fantastic themes of the paper projects balance the laconic and abstract of the project aspect which does not itself require a concrete reality imperative for proposing. Miniature-like, fantastic legends create a world in which the function and form of the projects become comprehensible. Of course, it is often unclear whether the project is determined by the legend, or the legend by the project. A similar ambivalence of the literary and architectural plans is characteristic of the romanticism of the late 18th century in which the utopias as well as the pictures of a "total environment" were created that today are regarded as the foundation of contextualism. The following is new for paper architecture: like literature it is capable of appropriating the open, ironic and romantic spirit of the theatrical, behind which other and no less essential foundations of the literary aspect of conceptual projects take shape – the reflecting upon language as a phenomenon of 20th century culture.

It is this reflecting upon language that devalues the totality of utopia and the claim to totality of the ideological programs. It is not merely a matter of the scientific reflecting upon language in the realm of linguistics and semiotics, although it is well-known how great their influence on modern architecture really is. Rather, we are talking about a broader cultural phenomenon: the loss of the magic power of words and its reversion into a simple agreed-upon meaning which is completely used as a lie. In place of the concept of language as a carrier of truth we find the notion that defines the word as follows: the word is something that lies.

The great magic of the word over which shamans and prophets in former centuries had command, which inspired the philosophers of the last century and is still inspiring the "Symbolists" in our century, also formed the basis of the utopian doctrines which are founded essentially on concepts and categories. This belief in linguistic constructions toppled not only under the pressure of dadaist irony, but rather under the burden of the totalitarian societies' demagogical structure which revealed the discrepancy between the word and the actual state of affairs. They forced everybody to pass off the desired (by whom? by the utopists?, by the powerful? by the architects?) as reality without experiencing even the least sensation of a romantic prophetic inspiration. The creative freedom is the freedom to use language in its agreed meanings. It can be accompanied by the open outburst of a romantic poet but can also be the friut of insensitive writing. Trite eulogies to the leaders and stagelike decorations for the bureacratic regime have divested language (the language of poetry as well as that of architecture) of its sacred meaning. The fact that one became aware of the independence of language from reality on the one hand, strenghtens the creative freedom of the use of language on the other hand, while nonetheless limiting its impact to the same degree. Creative activity is regarded as an occupation which can be designated by Wittgenstein's term: "chess games". These games can have totally serious traits or as H. Gadamer noted (continuing Heidegger's thought) only the games required total seriousness although they could also be dangerously irresponsible. Today's return to the language of classicism or constructivism is by no means supposed to instill fear – this is an ironic return, at most a play with classicism and constructivism, with which the state will hardly inferfere since it prefers games whose meaning has not yet been discovered.

Reflecting about the conditionality of language reduces the pathetic realization of the project to absurdity. The project becomes the "hypothesis" (L. Kahn). The hypothesis of the author, whose materialization in granite or reinforced concrete is not always appropriate, takes the place of the collective hypnosis through utopia. Reflecting upon language eliminates the symbolic power of the sign. According to Wittgenstein language reminds one of an "instrument case". If one looks at language from the archaic side then language is the equivalent of myth or truth, whereas from the angle of reflecting it is merely a collection of methods or a dependent code to which one does not have to submit. The place of the static symbol of language is taken by the dynamic symbol that is speech, which is neither equal to language nor separate from it. Literature is a kind of speech which is capable of evoking several possible worlds, among them the world of utopia. This freedom is greater than the mere absence of bureaucratic patronizing. The creation of worlds that are not meant to be totally realized is to some extent an irresponsible matter, to another a humorous thing.

It is possible, however, that Hegel was right when he assumed that everything sensible is also true. But does everything sensible have to be realized? The world is too small for all of the sensible ideas! And what should happen to the not altogether sensible or stupid ideas? Should they be forbidden? Or should their full realization be abandoned thereby to give them thousands of possibilities? To me the second idea seems preferable.

To save the projects from this condemnation to which we have come pretty close, we probably have to learn to renounce the realization of the projects. Theoretical design has reawakened the parable of the sorcerer's apprentice whose broom followed his every command. The establishment of order in conformance with all possible worlds would lead to greater chaos than that which existed before designing.

The rejection of realization, however, does not mean a rejection of reality. One of the most radical problems surfaces here. What is the reality that is dependent neither on a design proposition nor on fantasy; does it really exist? It is easy to break with socialist realism as a system, one that does not comply with the multifaceted living reality. It is difficult to find a criterion capable of separating wish from truth, fantasy from reality, future from present, mask from face, in short — to depict reality. Perhaps there is no reality that is not closely linked to fantasy, no truth that is not dependent on a proposition or a norm. It is not reality which should be put in the center but truth should be identified; a means should be sought that can create a connecting link between man, his life, his existence and the concomitant truth.

One truth should not be forced under the pressure of seduction by advertisement or by the threat of reprisals to take the place of another truth, but a possible connection has to be found, a dialogue of possible worlds and projects. This task can only be solved by a simple confontation: past and future, natural and artificical, order and chaos, East and West etc.; a solution will only be possible if an honest and free exchange of thoughts and ideas can be reached between these opposites.

Communication is not limited to conversation between people although, such conversation is the basis of communication. The conversation of the individual "Egos" among themselves is also a prerequisite for communication. It may be that the cooperation of individuals and their wishes and projects behind them will develop through this process.

If cooperation is understood in this way (one that does not contradict the professional or economic cooperation that is a constituent of the vocabulary of architects) it may reveal the meaning of concepts that have not yet been devalued by reflecting upon language. And — let us permit ourselves a little utopia — what happens when language devalued by reflecting returns to the condition in which the reality of things is the word and the authenticity of life is the basis for architecture?

PAPER ARCHITECTURE

E. Ass, City Nr. 2, 1979—1984
Gouache, 24 × 24 cm

19

Veduta della citta № 2

1 Башня номер один
2 большой портик
3 penthouses

4. наверное спуск в метро
5. почта-телеграф-телефон
6. ресторан „citta"

7. Семен Григорьевич
8. магазин „Вино"
9. дом № 17 по ул. Героев

E. Ass, City Nr. 2, 1979—1984
Indian ink, paper, 28 × 19,3 cm

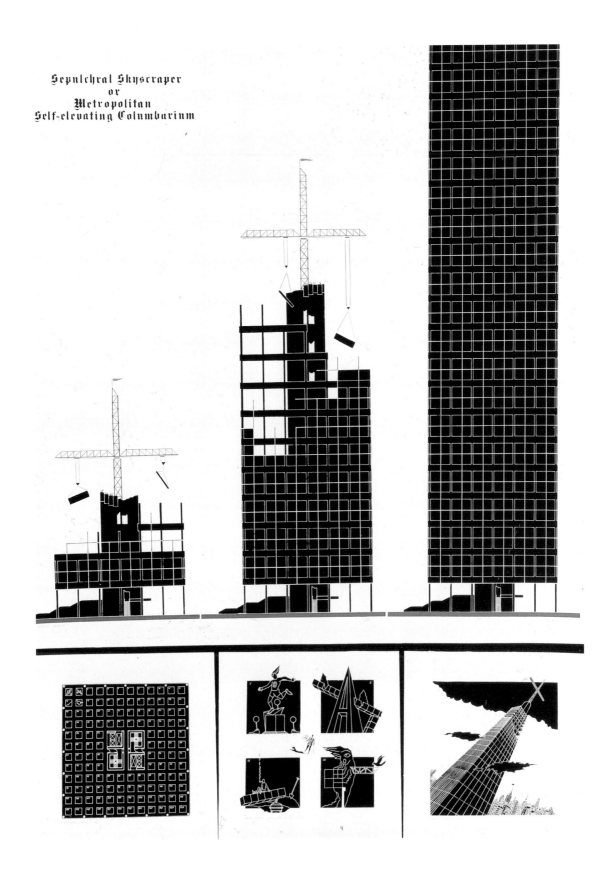

Sepulchral Skyscraper
or
Metropolitan
Self-elevating Columbarium

Y. Awwakumov, M. Belov, Sepulchral Skyscraper, 1983
Fotocopy, 84 × 60 cm

Y. Awwakumov, S. Podyomshchikov, Self-erecting Prefabricated Playhouse, 1983
Playing cards, 90 × 24 × 24 cm

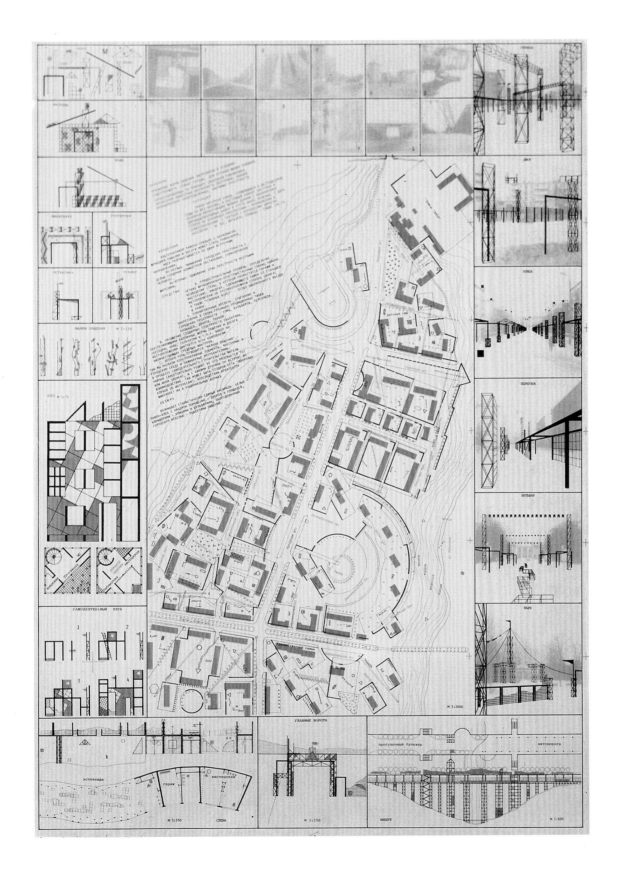

Y. Awwakumov, SACB of the Moscow Architectural Institute, A City of Clubs, 1984
Engraving, 82 × 59 cm

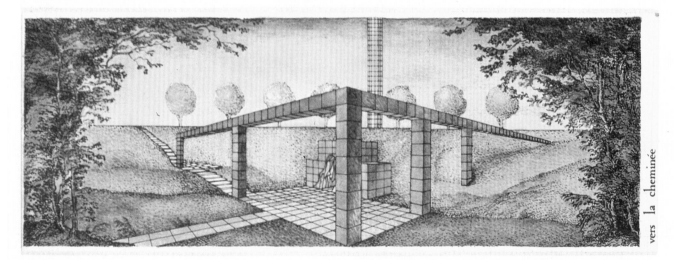

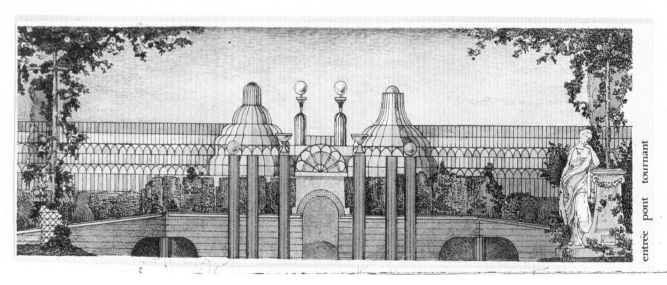

Y. Awwakumov, M. Belov, B. Jerjomin, W. Lomakin, I. Lechava, La Villette, 1984
Aquarelle, offset print 67 × 95 cm

24

Y. Awwakumov, T. Kuzembayev, I. Pitchukevich, Informcity, 1986
Engraving, 84 × 60 cm

25

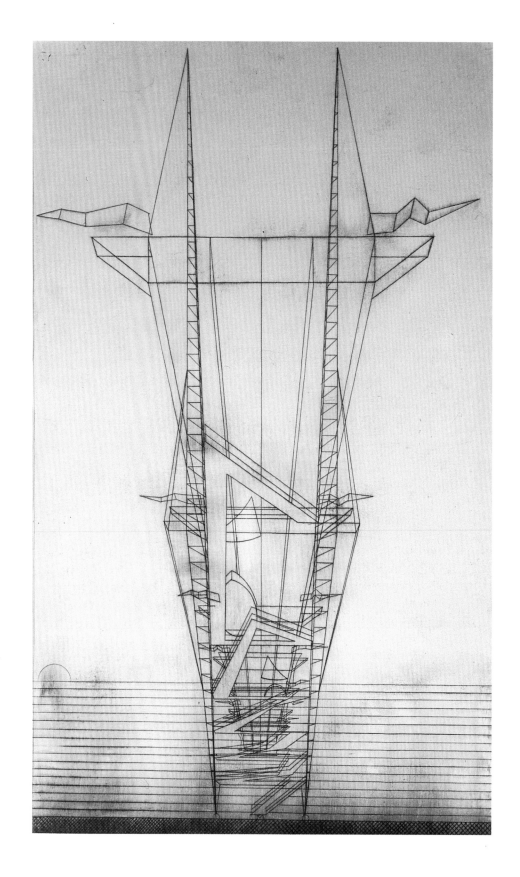

Y. Awwakumov, J. Kuzin, Bridge over the Wall, 1987
Engraving, 84 × 60 cm

26

Y. Awwakumov, J. Kuzin, S. Podyomshchikov, Red Tower, 1988
Model: metal, 64 × 29 × 29 cm

A. Baldin, The Babylonian Tower, 1987
Indian ink, paper, 62 × 40 cm

S. Barkhin, M. Belov, G. Solopov, The Street of the Architect (Reconstruction of Shusev street in Moscow), 1987
Indian ink, paper, 100 × 140 cm

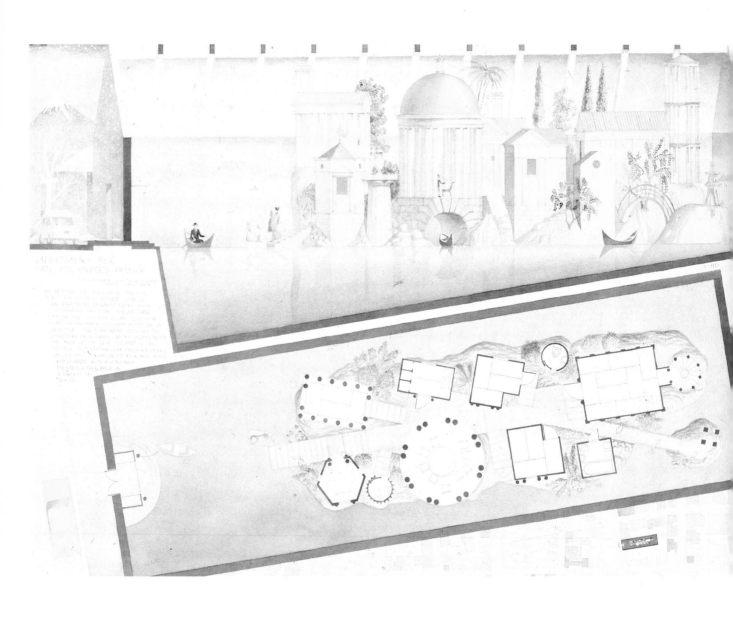

S. Barkhin, M. Belov, A Japanese House or a Dwelling for an Islander's Family, 1987
Aquarelle and pencil, paper, 60 × 84 cm

L. Batalov, D. Zaitsev, Abode of Memory, 1988
Model: Lumber, mirror, acrillic plastic glass, 30 × 50 × 50 cm

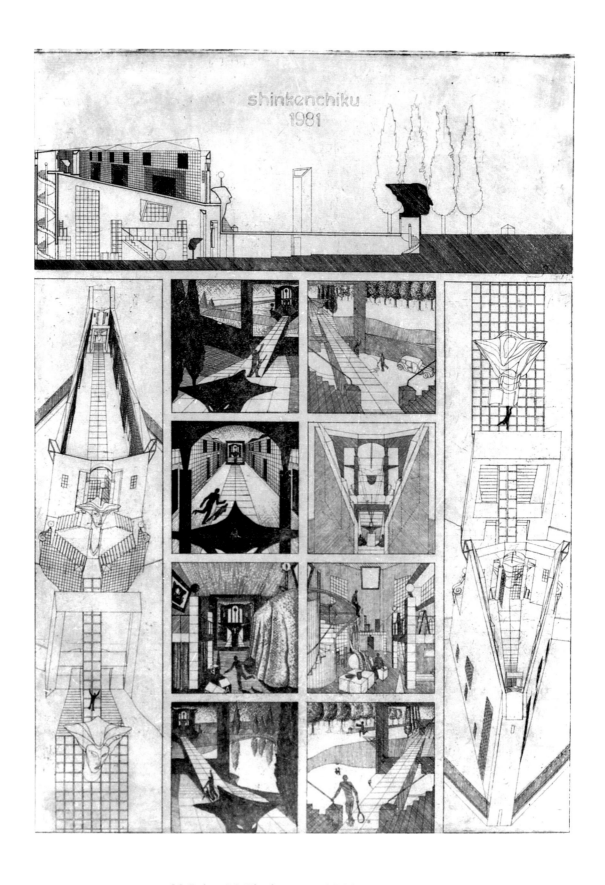

M. Belov, M. Kharitonov, Exhibition House, 1981
Etching, 70 × 50 cm

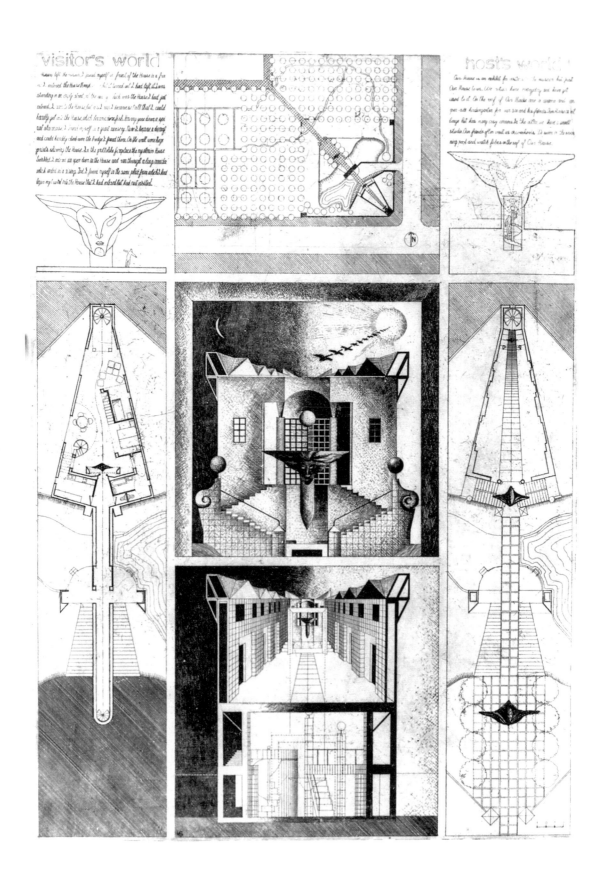

M. Belov, M. Kharitonov, Exhibition House, 1981
Etching, 70 × 50 cm

33

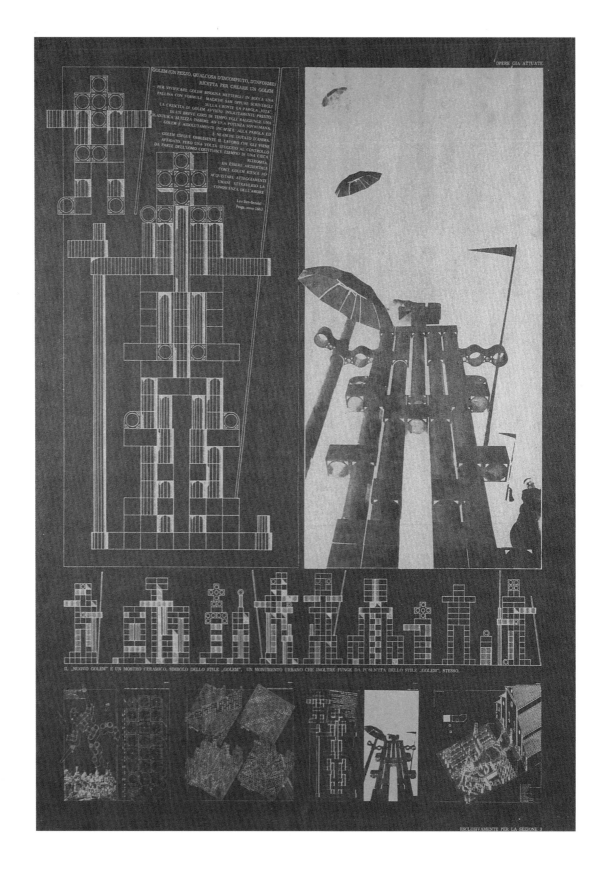

M. Belov, M. Krikhely, I. Pitschukevich, D. Airapetov, Golem, 1983
Offset print, 70 × 50 cm

M. Belov, Bridge across the Rubicon, 1987
Mixed technique, 86 × 60 cm

M. Belov, Tokyo National Theatre, 1987
Indian ink, Aquarelle, paper, 60 × 84 cm

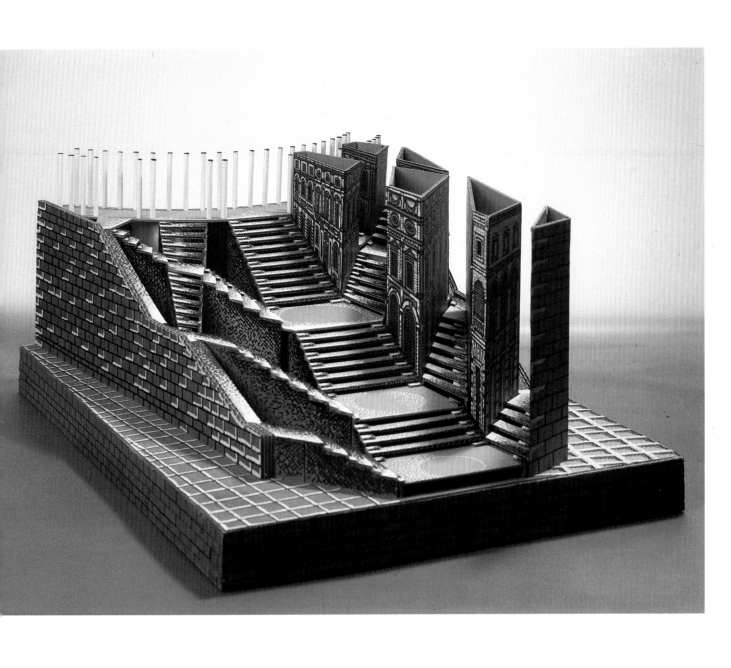

M. Belov, M. Khazanov, New Teatro Olimpico, 1987—1988
Model, 35 × 50 × 70 cm

37

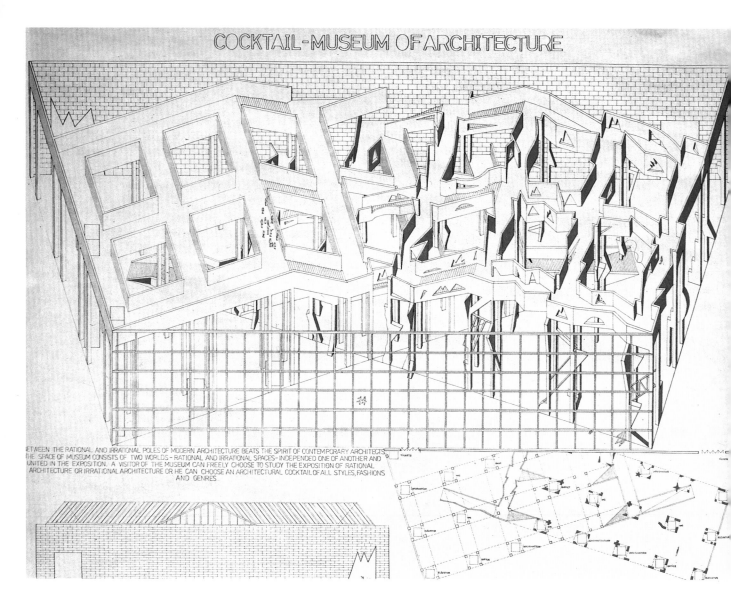

BETWEEN THE RATIONAL AND IRRATIONAL POLES OF MODERN ARCHITECTURE BEATS THE SPIRIT OF CONTEMPORARY ARCHITECTS. THE SPACE OF MUSEUM CONSISTS OF TWO WORLDS – RATIONAL AND IRRATIONAL SPACES– INDEPENDED ONE OF ANOTHER AND UNITED IN THE EXPOSITION. A VISITOR OF THE MUSEUM CAN FREELY CHOOSE TO STUDY THE EXPOSITION OF RATIONAL ARCHITECTURE OR IRRATIONAL ARCHITECTURE OR HE CAN CHOOSE AN ARCHITECTURAL COCKTAIL OF ALL STYLES, FASHIONS AND GENRES.

M. Belov, Museum of Architecture, 1988
60 × 64 cm

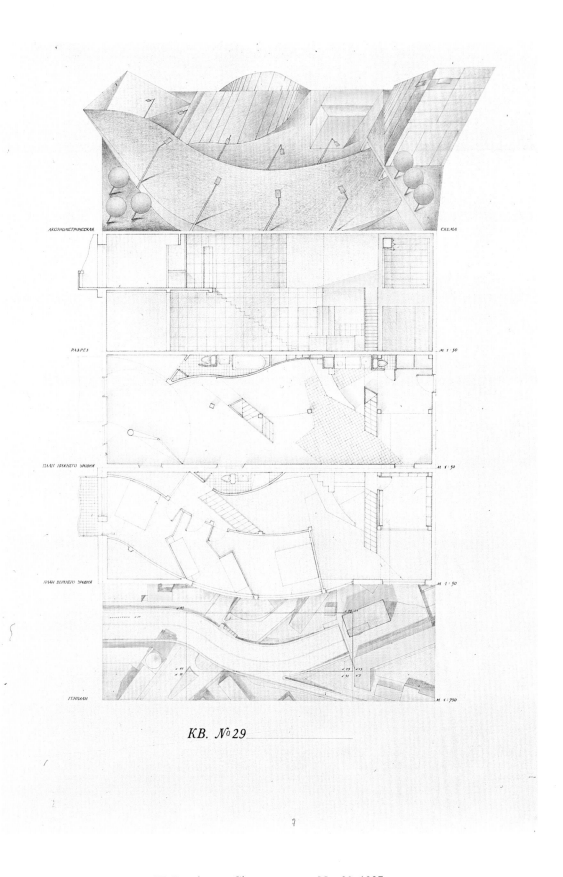

W. Bogdanov, City-apartment No. 29, 1987
Indian ink, paper, 84 × 60

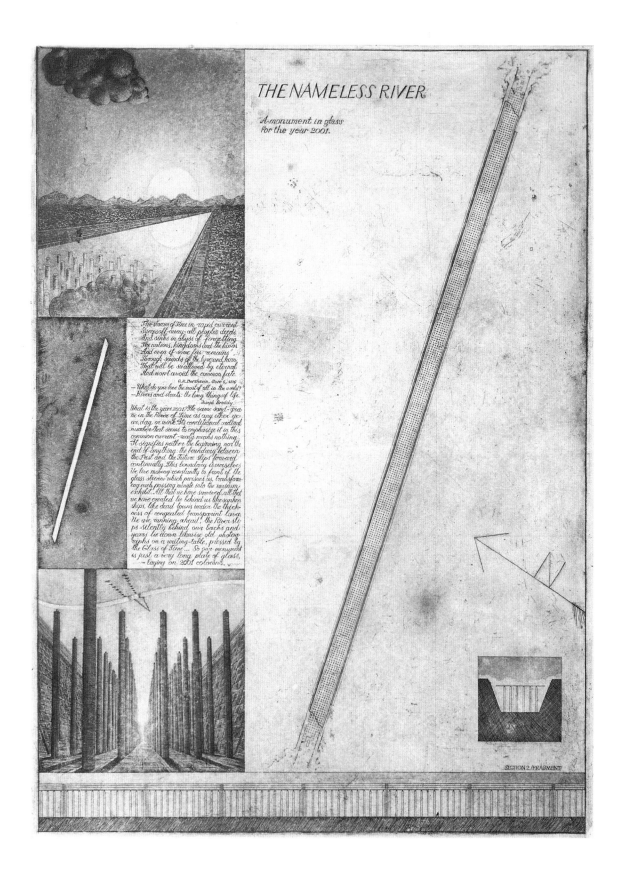

A. Brodsky, I. Utkin, The Nameless River, 1986
Etching, 79,1 × 69,6 cm

A. Brodsky, I. Utkin, House, 1986
Etching, 40,5 × 28 cm

41

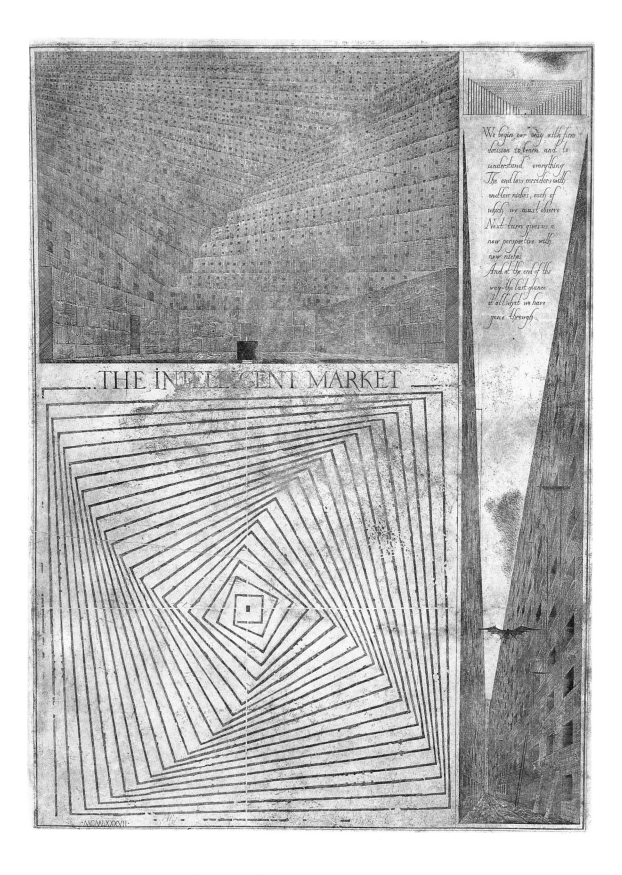

The Intelligent Market

We begin our way with firm
decision to learn and to
understand everything
The endless corridors with
endless niches, each of
which we must observe
Next turn gives us a
new perspective with
new niches
And at the end of the
way-the last glance
at all what we have
gone through

MCMLXXXVII

A. Brodsky, I. Utkin, The Intelligent Market, 1987
Etching, 70,6 × 54,3 cm

A. Brodsky, I. Utkin, Museum of Architecture and Contemporary Art, 1987
Etching, 73,5 × 59 cm

A. Brodsky, I. Utkin, A Bridge above the Precipice, 1987
Etching, 75 × 55,3 cm

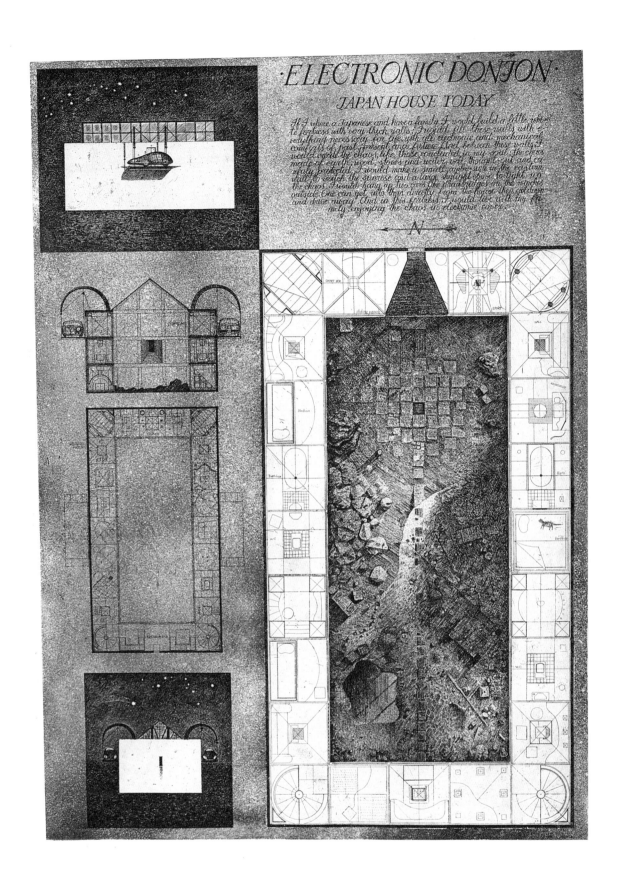

A. Brodsky, I. Utkin, Electronic Dungeon, 1987
Etching, 74,3 × 54,8 cm

A. Brodsky, I. Utkin, Man-City, 1988
Modell: plaster, 54 × 32 × 41 cm

A. Brodsky, I. Utkin, Ship of Fools or Wooden Skycraper for a Jolly Company, 1988
Etching, 74,5 × 56 cm

N. Bronzova, Spice-and-Honey-Cake House, 1984
Indian ink, Aquarelle, paper, 85 × 65 cm

N. Bronzova, Spice-and-Honey-Cake House, 1984
Model: paste, 40 × 40 × 36

N. Bronzova, M. Filippov, Museum of Sculpture, 1983
Aquarelle, 26 × 55 (2)

N. Bronzova, M. Filippov, Noah's Ark, 1987
Aquarelle, 50 × 70 cm

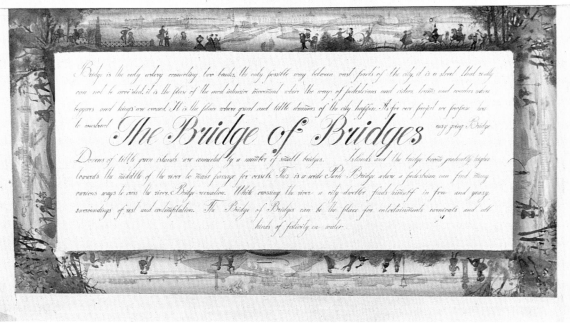

N. Bronzova, M. Filippov, The Bridge of Bridges, 1987
Indian ink and Aquarelle, paper, 85 × 60 cm

M. Filippov, The Window, 1988
Aquarelle

БЕСКОНЕЧНОСТЬ В КУБЕ

КАЖДАЯ КВАРТИРА ВЫХОДИТ В ЗЕРКАЛЬНОЕ ПРОСТРАНСТВО ВНУТРЕННЕГО ДВОРА
СРЕДИ ГОРОДСКОГО ХАОСА КРИСТАЛЛИЗУЕТСЯ ЧИСТАЯ БЕСКОНЕЧНОСТЬ

РАЗРЕЗ

ПЛАН

D. Busch, D. Podyapolsky, A. Khomyakov, The Cube of Infinity, 1986
Serigraphy, 60 × 84 cm

54

D. Busch, D. Podyapolsky, A. Khomyakov, High Mountains, 1986
Indian ink, paper, 70 × 50 cm

D. Busch, Khomyakov, Glass Stonehenge, 1986
Indian ink, paper, 84 × 60 cm

D. Busch, D. Podyapolsky, A. Khomyakov, Interplay, 1984/88
Plastics, mirrored glass, 50 × 50 × 50 cm

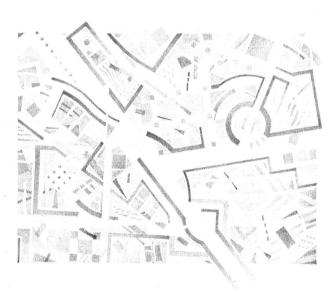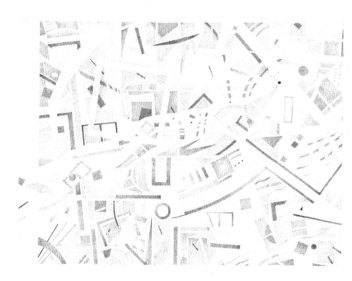

A. Dmitriev, Architectural Vision, 1978/88
Indian ink, paper, 36 × 48 cm each

D. Busch, D. Podyapolsky, A. Khomyakov, Mon Plaisir, 1985
Serigraphy, 84 × 60 cm

I. Galimov, Temple-City, 1988
Indian ink, paper, 60 × 84 cm

60

A. Gutnov, B. Levyant, S. Lobachev, I. Shalmin, Unity of Nations Palace, 1985
Xerocopy, colored paper, 45 × 39 cm

N. Kaverin, O. Kaverina, Design for the City Man's Second Dwelling, 1985
Indian ink and pencil 12,5 × 58,5 cm, 26 × 29 (2×) cm, 38,8 × 28,8 (2×) cm

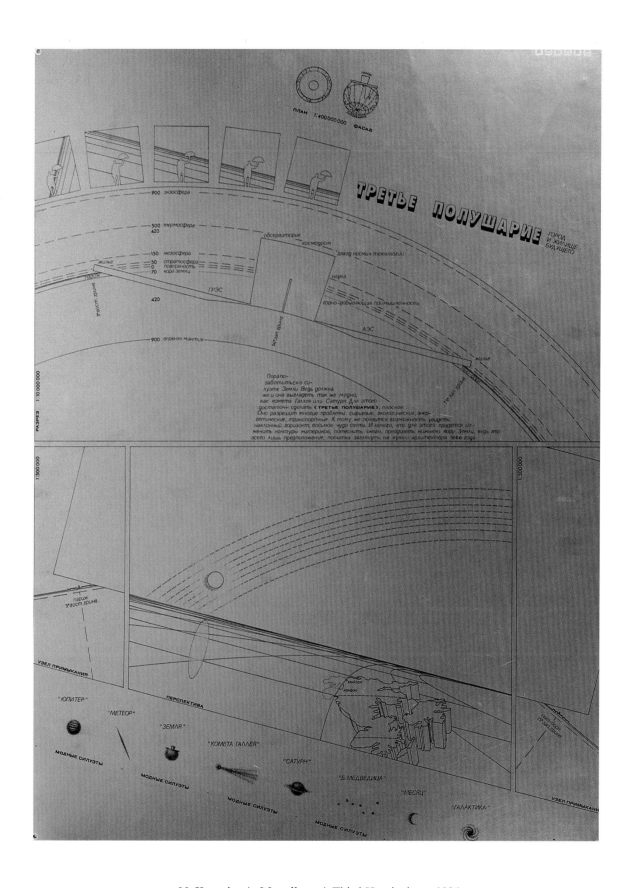

N. Kaverin, A. Myznikov, A Third Hemisphere, 1986
Metallized paper, Indian ink, 78,5 × 58,5 cm

V. Khodnev, Y. Kostina, Theater with a Belvedere, 1988
Tracing paper, Indian ink, colored pencils, 86 × 60 cm

M. Korolkov, D. Shelest, M. Belov, Gallery Concord, 1985
Pencil, paper, 84 × 60 cm

65

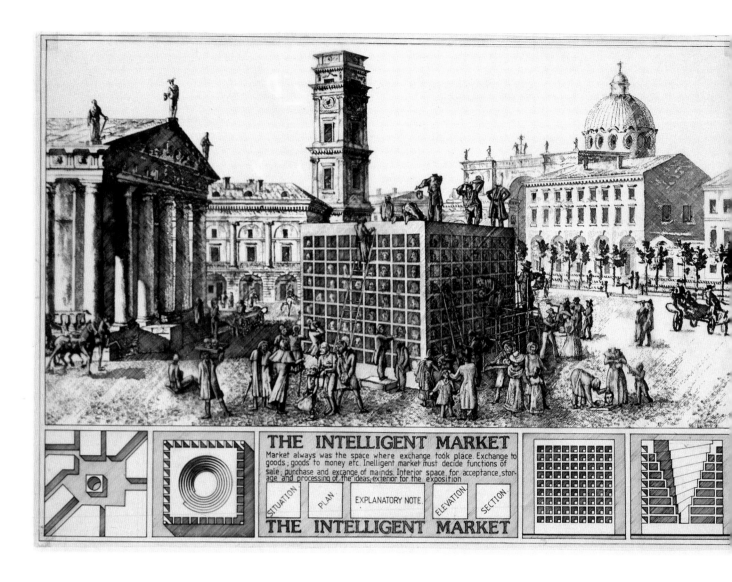

A. Krupin, A. Miroshin, V. Tregubova, The Intelligent Market, 1987
Indian ink, synthetic tracing paper, 58,2 × 83 cm

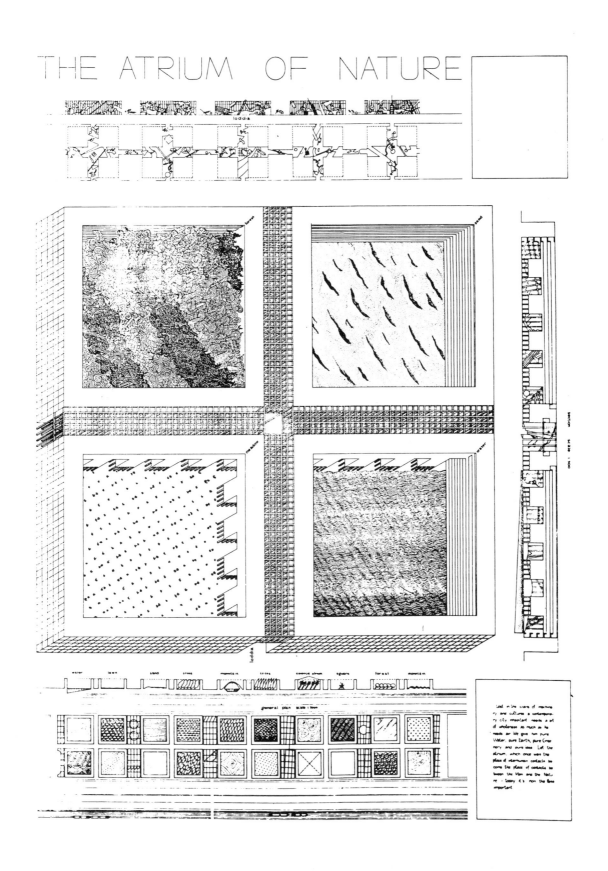

THE ATRIUM OF NATURE

T. Kuzembayev, A. Ivanov, V. Aristov, Bulwark of Resistance, 1985
Xerography, Indian ink, 84 × 60 cm

67

T. Kuzembayev, A. Ivanov, W. Aristov, Dwelling for Tomorrow, 1984
Fotocopy, Aquarelle, 69 × 48 cm

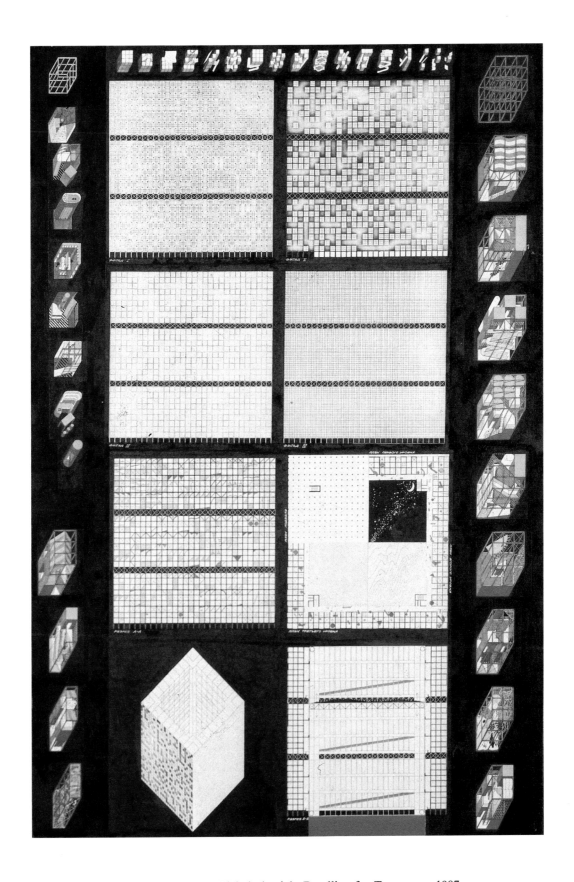

T. Kuzembayev, I. Pishchukevich, Dwelling for Tomorrow, 1987
Indian ink and Gouache, paper, 84 × 60 cm

T. Kuzembayev, I. Pishchukevich, Dwelling of the Future, 1988
Model: wood, glass, metal, 64 × 46 × 20 cm

Y. Kuzin, Shanghai, 1987
Mixed technique, 89 × 57 cm

71

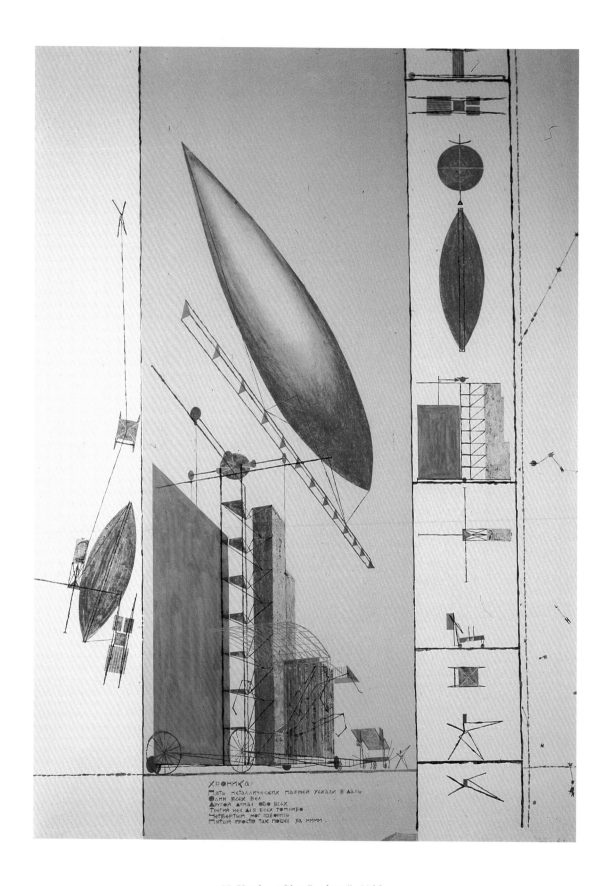

Y. Kuzin, "City Sockets", 1988
Oil, plastic, 100 × 70 cm

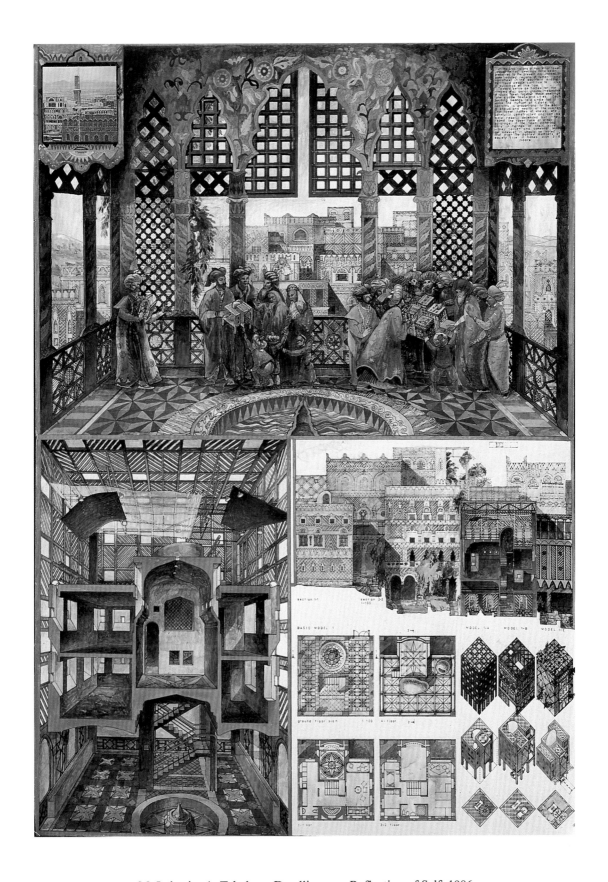

M. Labasin, A. Tshelsov, *Dwelling as a Reflection of Self*, 1986
Aquarelle, photographic paper, varnish, 82 × 56,5 cm

73

M. Labazov, A. Savvin, Genius Loci, 1984
Photofabric, 80 × 60 cm

M. Labazov, A. Tchelzov, A. Savvin, Dwelling Today, 1988
Model: wood, plaster, 47 × 50 × 50 cm

75

театр индивидуального Восприятия

1 ячейка – 1 человек

L. Pavlov, M. Bartenev, V. Shteller, N. Gorkin, Personal Perception Theater, 1978
Indian ink, paper, 60 × 80 cm

W. Petrenko, Reflections over the Theme, 1981
Etching, 110 × 70 cm

S. Resnikov, Cubism, 1979
Pencil, paper, 36 × 64 cm

S. Resnikov, White House, 1983
Pencil, paper, 36 × 64 cm

3/9

S. Resnikov, Winter Landscape, 1984
Lithography, 20 × 33 cm

A. Rodinov, Postindustrial Nest, 1986
Model: plaster, metal 40 × 50 × 50 cm

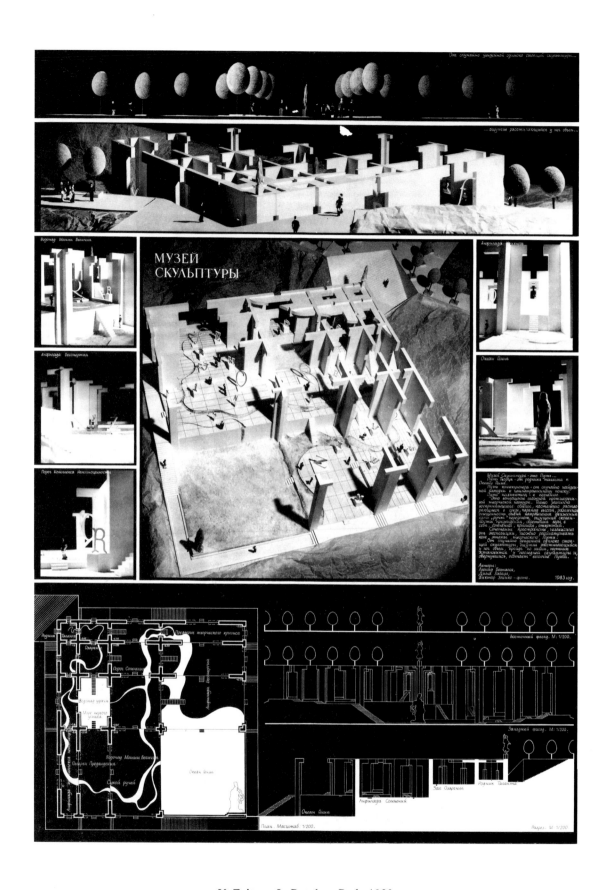

V. Zaitsev, L. Batalov, Path, 1983
Photocollage, 84 × 60 cm

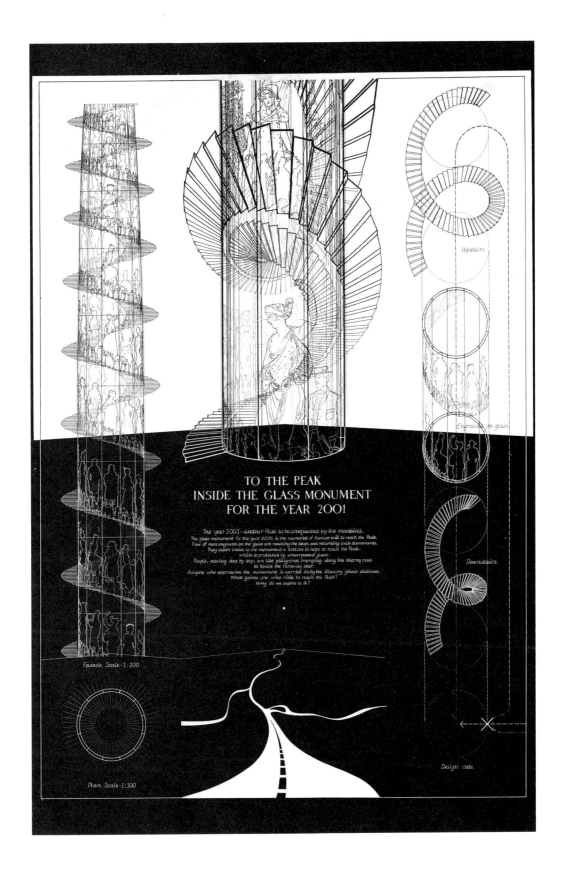

V. Zaitsev, L. Batalov, Rising to the Peak, 1986
Tempera, paper, 84 × 60 cm

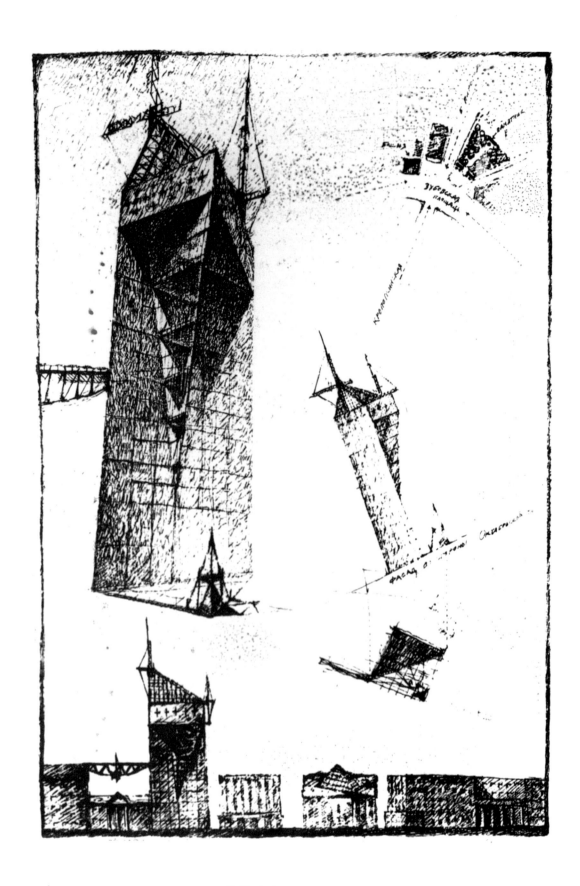

I. Shalmin, Tower, 1986
Serigraphy, 42 × 30 cm

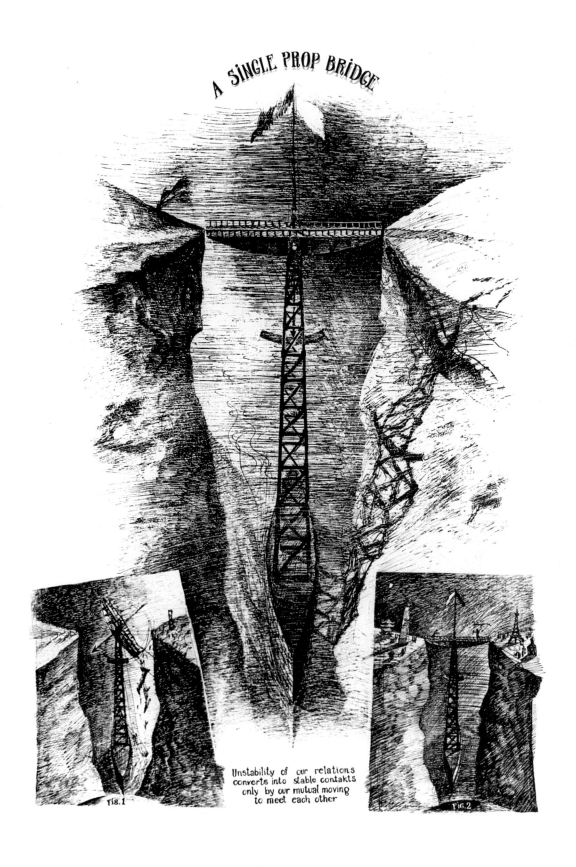

I. Shalmin, Single-Pier Bridge, 1987
Serigraphy, 100 × 70 cm

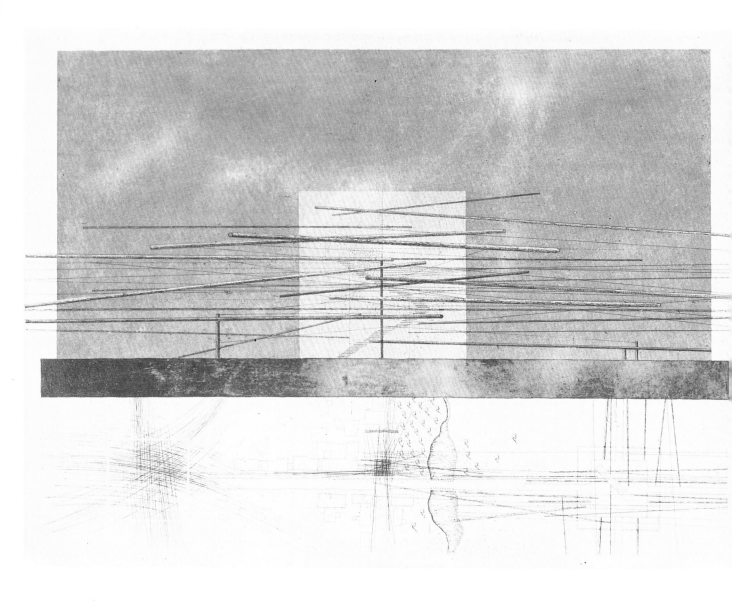

A. Savvin, Space, 1987
Etching, 48 × 63 cm

D. Shelest, A. Shelest, Cross-Country Cottage, 1985
Xerocopy, 84 × 60 cm

ГОРОДСКОЕ ПРОСТРАНСТВО БУДУЩЕГО

A. Sigatchev, 21st-Century Space, 1988
Aquarelle, Gouache, 84 × 60 cm

A. Sosimov, Architecture, 1986/87
Collage, 11 × 21,4 cm

W. Turin, The Intelligent Market, 1987
Indian ink, Aquarelle, 84 × 59,4 cm

A. Cheltsov, M. Labazov, Aquarium City, 1987
Aquarelle, 59,5 × 40 cm

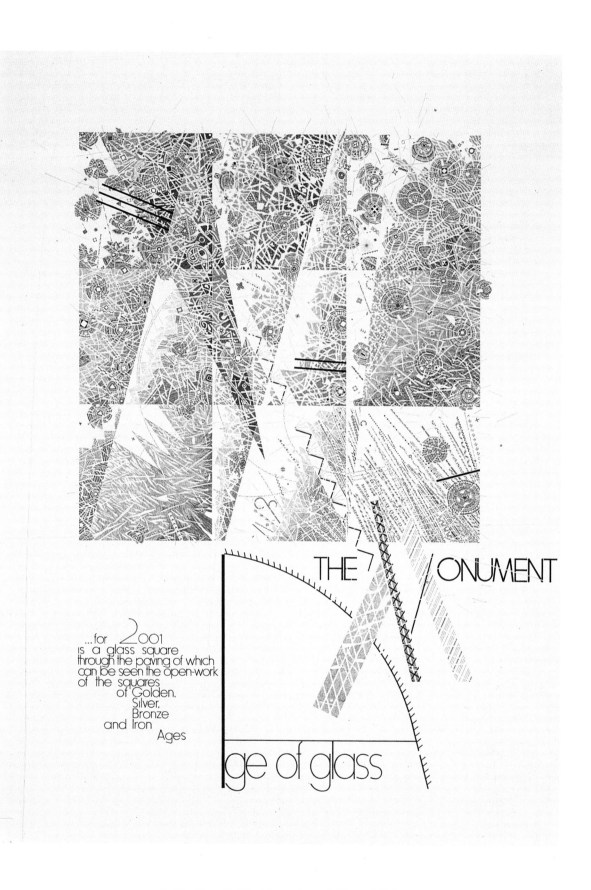

THE /ONUMENT

...for 2001
is a glass square
through the paving of which
can be seen the open-work
of the squares
of Golden,
Silver,
Bronze
and Iron
Ages

ge of glass

S. Chuklov, V. Chuklova, Age of Glass, 1986
Serigraphy, 84 × 60 cm

92

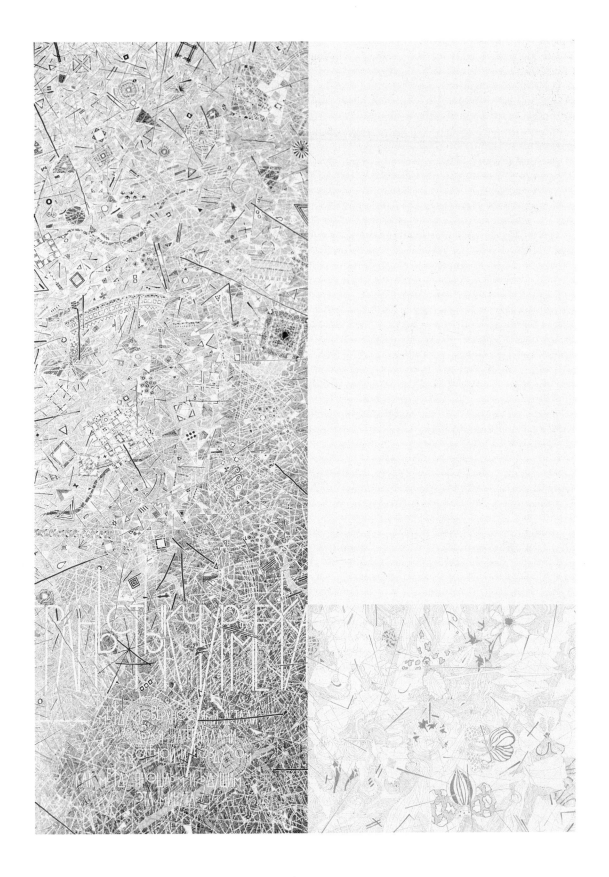

S. Chuklov, V. Chuklova, Edge-Junction-Limit-Boundary, 1987
Indian ink, paper, 84 × 60 cm

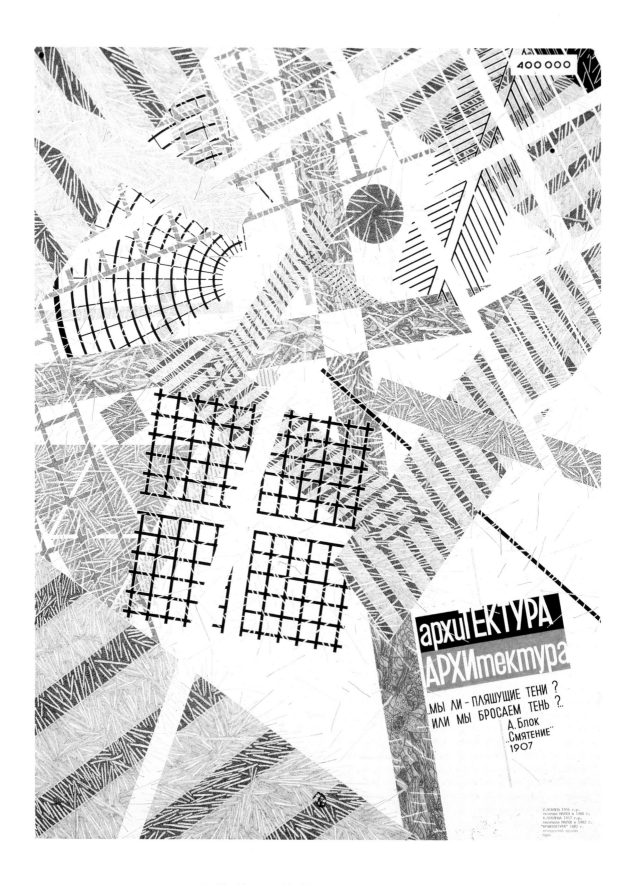

S. Chuklov, V. Chuklova, Architecture, 1987
Indian ink, Gouache, paper, 80 × 60 cm

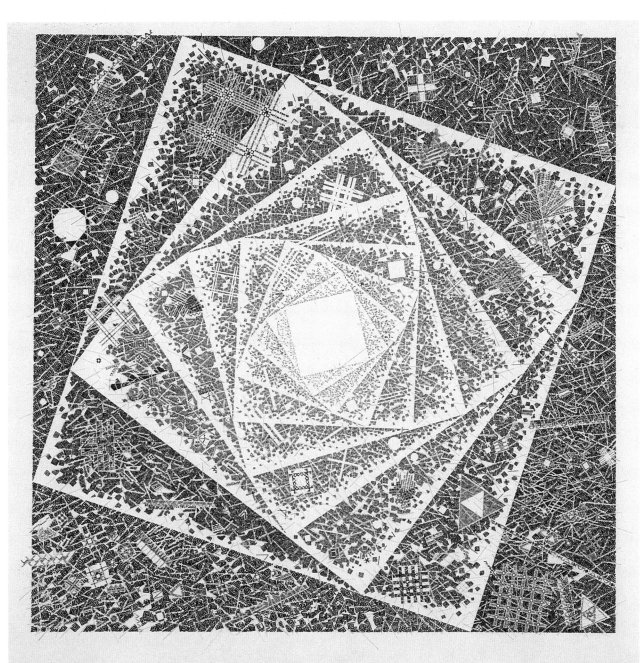

WHILE DEEPER PENETRATING INTO THE NATURE,
WE LEAVE BEHIND US A GEOMETRICAL LANDSCAPE.
XXI CENTURY : THE STONE, THROWN INTO THE WATER,
MAKES SQUARES.

S. Chuklov, V. Chuklova, A Stone Cast into the Water, 1988
Indian ink, paper, 84 × 60 cm

D. Velichkin, V. Levi, D. Shelest, Camera-Museum, 1983
Pencil, paper, 84 × 60 cm

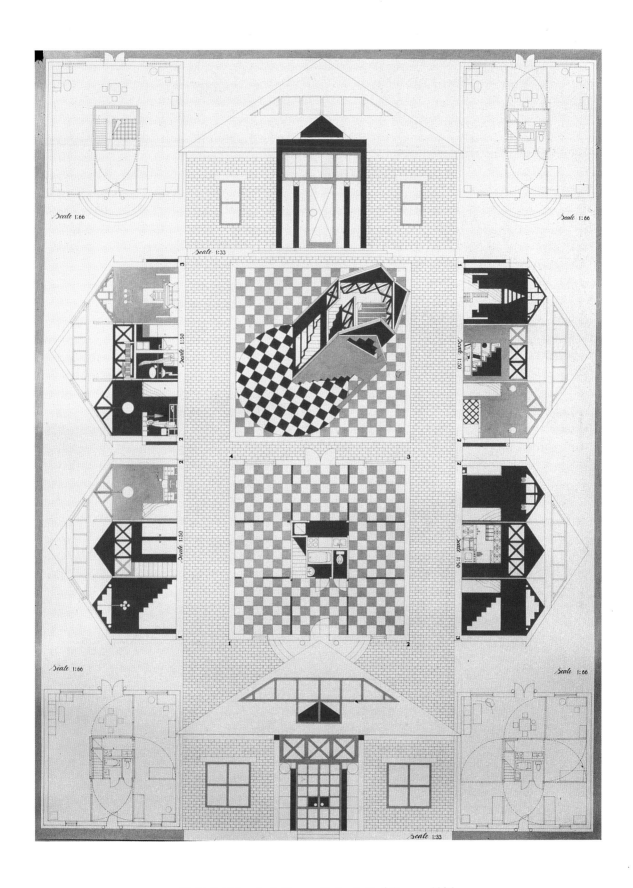

D. Velichkin, A. Bel'ayev, V. Levi, Red Tower, 1986
Indian ink, tempera, paper, 84 × 61 cm

97

V. Voronova, A. Ignatyev, A. Petrov, Center for Leisure-Time Activities and Communication, 1984
Indian ink, paper, 80 × 60 cm

V. Voronova, A. Ignatyev, A. Petrov, One day Atrium, 1985
Aquarell, pencil, paper, 59 × 19,5

99

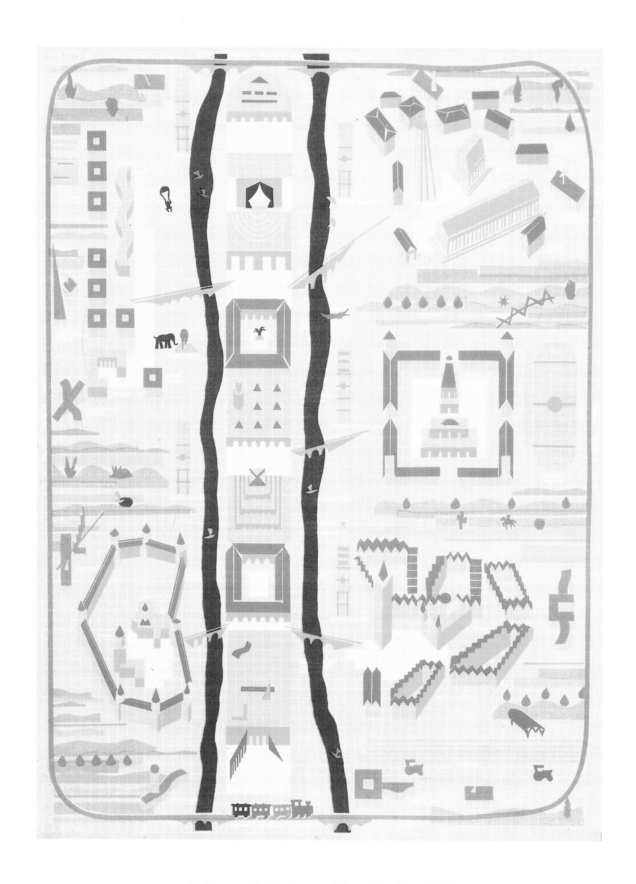

V. Vorona, O. Brezlavzeva, City of the Wise, 1987
Etching, 73 × 55 cm

100

Project Descriptions

This object symbolizes modern architectural technology. It has a certain degree of independence from the architect. The model is on a scale of 1:12. To make the model you need cards, adhesive tape and pieces of rubber. It is simultaneously a children's toy of the Jack-in-the-Box type and a theater structure.

The Problem as seen in 1984
Conditions in the existing town make ordinary forms of social intercourse difficult. A certain chaos in building and an abundance of functionally undetermined, amorphous spaces are characteristic of large housing neighborhoods projected on the principle of free planning.

The Situation
The neighborhood of a sloping street created south of Moscow in the 1960s at present contains 8 five-story apartment buildings interspersed with twelve-story towers and has a dense green cover. On two sides it is bounded by thoroughfares, the Nakhimovsky and Sevastopolsky Avenues, and on the third side by a trench-like ravine. The population is 30,000, and the area is over 100 hectares.

The Concept
As an alternative, the bedtown-zone with undeveloped functions for social exchange and amusement could become a club region. The idea was developed in two opposite directions.
First, closing up urban spaces with the aim of creating a comfortable situation on the human scale.
Second, settling these spaces with local inhabitants.

The Means
A. On the urban development level.
Establishing clear functional-spatial boundaries of the neighborhood. Building a wall in which garages and shops will be located. Building a viaduct to connect the neighborhood with the subway station on the opposite side of the ravine. Building so-called Main Gates which will have distinctive forms and serve as the entrance to the neighborhood.

B. On the planning level. Discovering and strengthening traditional urban spaces within their own boundaries: streets, boulevards, alleys, squares, courts and parks.

C. Filling the spaces created with objects affording all kinds of social intercourse and amusement: belvederes, cafes, pigeon houses and so forth. The selection of their placement is dictated by the entire complex of mediating factors.

A special role goes to Contact Beacons, or elements introduced in the urban sphere and brought to life by the inhabitants. In the process of independent construction, the residents of the neighborhood decide on their own of which constituent elements every larger element should consist and how it should cooperate with other elements. For instance, a network of court clubs arranged according to the interests of the residents could be created. Later an architect could fix these elements in rational forms.

Resume for the year 2001
A stylistically unified ensemble will result from this approach: an club neighborhood with a choice of facilities: courts, squares, corridors, streets, and boulevards-all outfitted with urban furnishings-objects of human relations and contact.

The Intelligent Plaza is the primary element of urban sociospatial reconstruction.
The Intelligent Plaza combines ordinary everyday activities with totally new activities and with ordinary activities in a new environment.

The Intelligent Plaza arises when new activities are added to already existing ones, and subsequently provoke a clash of unrelated activities which can lead to the emergence of even more forms of urban activity.

The Intelligent Plaza is not a finished structure: its activities can develop, change and even vanish, and its name can be altered should a new activity take precedence over a previous one.

The Intelligent Plaza is a combination of spaces of varying size, intended for individual, group and mass activities.

The Intelligent Plaza defines its own spaces by means of a system of barriers, both visual and physical.

The Intelligent Plaza defines excludes the theatrical principle of perception. Information is not a specific object on the Plaza, but the Plaza as a whole represents a source of information.

The Intelligent Plaza represents agriculture, science and industry through three groups of symbols, the interpretation of which depends on their urban context.

The Intelligent Plaza attempts to combine the city of the past and the city of the present and future via traditional signs and ideograms.

A Teach-yourself City

This way, the programmed interconnection between the symbolic, the spatial and the functional in each plaza, apart from being a simple combination of spaces, functions and situations comprehensible to everyone, also trains everyones ability to synthesize these three elements into a single symbolic urban formation. The Intelligent Plaza is intended to educate people to identify with the city, take part in its formation and construction, as well as to become significant elments in the urban process.

Page 26
Y. Awwakumow, Y. Kuzin, *Bridge Across the Wall,* 1987

"One might build a little bridge across the abyss" (E. Zamiatin)

The wall is the gap full of human prejudice, garbage, traffic jams and political arguments.

The Sunrise Bridge across the wall connects the past and the present, the East and the West, nature and city, fantasy and reality.

The bridge is moving along the wall. The upper edge of the bridge is the sky and the sun is its sails; the middle part consists of floating islands inhabited by people; and the lowest part is the river with an artificial wave.

Page 30
S. Barkhin, M. Belov, *A Japanese House or a Dwelling for an Islander's Family*
JA Competition, 1987 2nd Prize

"All the Japanese love their island."
(From a geography book)

A dwelling for a present-day Japanese family may be an apartment in which every room is a separate pavilion standing in a Japanese garden. Together they form an ensemble designed in accordance with ancient traditions on a 170-square-meter rocky island washed by a rectangular freshwater lake surrounded by a brick wall and covered by a glass roof.

The proposed location is any unoccupied space in a Tokyo neighborhood.

Page 31
L. Batalow, D. Zaitsev, *Abode of Memory,* 1988
JA Competition Chrystal Palace, Honorable Mention

Thy bosom is endeared will all hearts,
Which I by lacking have supposed dead;
And there reigns love, and all love's loving parts,
And all those friends which I tought buried.
How many a holy and obsequious tear
Hath dear-religious love stol'n from mine eye,
As interest of the dead, which now appear
But things remov'd, that hidden in thee lie!
Thou art the grave where buried love doth live.
Hung with the trophies of my lovers gone,
Who all their parts of me to thee did give;
That due of many now is thine alone:
Their images I lov'd I view in thee,
And thou, all they, hast all the all of me.

William Shakespeare
Sonnet 31

Page 32/33
V. Belov, M. Kharitonov, *Exhibition House on the Grounds of the 20th-Century Museum*
JA Competition, 1981, 1st Prize

Visitor's World

Having left the museum, I found myself in front of the House in a frame. I entered the House through the frame, but it turned out that I had left it. I was standing in an empty street at the end of which there was the House I had just entered. I ran to the House, but as I ran I became so tall that I could hardly get into the House which became dwarfish. Having gone down a spiral staircase, I found myself in a giant nursery. Now I became a dwarf and could hardly climb over the bridge I found there. Huge prints showing the House were on the walls. The mysterious House twinkled in the grotto-like fireplace. I went through an open door inside the House and ran down a long corridor which ended in a rise. I found myself in the same place from which I had begun my trip into the House that I had entered but not visited.

Host's World
Our House is an exhibit for visitors but it is just Our House to us. We return here every day and have become used to it. There is a cinema and an open-air kindergarten for our son and his friends on the roof of Our House. Our House is not large but it has many cosy corners. In the attic, we have a small studio. Our friends often visit us on weekends. We swim in the swimming pool and watch films on the roof of Our House.

Page 34
Mikhail Belov, Mikhail Krikhely, Igor Pitschukevich (Dir. Dmitry Airapetov), *Golem,* 1983
Communa Di Facena Competition, Italy, Honorable Mention

1. Proposals for the output of ceramic elements
A set of standardized articles made of dense ceramics (designed in the GOLEM style) is proposed for a sectional ceramic urban design. The assembly is carried out without mortar on a structure of ceramic pipes.
2. Proposals for the use of ceramic materials
The possibilities of the set for creating an environment (in the GOLEM style).
3. Performing the job
The new golem is a ceramic monster, a symbol of the GOLEM style and an urban monument. It is also an advertisement of the GOLEM style in ceramics.
4. The recipe for creating a golem
To create a Golem you should take clay, model a figure having the height of a ten-year-old boy and put a magic ball, or SHAM (Life), in its mouth.
The creature will thus be endowed with life and begin to grow rapidly, reaching the height of a giant and the strength of an otherworldly being. However, if you lose control over the monster it will become disobedient and wander through the town, scaring passers-by. Should this happen, you must try and take away the magic SHAM ball after which the creature will abide in love and collapse, scattering ceramic fragments about town.
Ben Bezalelle
Prague, 1663

Page 39
V. Bogdanov, *City-apartment No.29,* 1987

The building is a city plan folded like the bellow of an accordion. Each of the resulting rectangles is an apartment. One of them is a small fragment of urban space, or apartment No.29.
An expressway passes through bedrooms.
The bathroom is behind a mirror facade of an office.
The cobbled square with an open-air cafe serves as a dining-room.
The kitchen is in the house across the street.
Cupboards from the perspective of the street.
All this will be seen espacially well if you step on your balcony.
That high tower in the distance is a clock in the neighbouring apartment No.351407.

Page 40
A. Brodsky, I. Utkin, *The Nameless River*
JA competition A Glass Monument for the Year 2001, 1986

The Nameless River

The stream of Time in rapid current
Sweeps off and away all people's deeds
And sinks in abbyss of forgetting
The nations, kingdoms and the kings.
And even if some of them remain
Thanks to the sounds of lyre and horn
They will be swallowed by eternity
And shan't avoid the common fate.
G.R. Derzhavin June 6, 1816

- What do you love the most of all in the world?
- Rivers and streets: the long things of life. J. Brodsky

What is the year 2001? It is the same sand grain in the River of Time, just like any other year, day or week. Its conditional ordinal number really means nothing. It signifies neither the beginning nor the end of anything: the boundary between the Past and the Future slips forward continually. This boundary is ourselves. We live and we move perpetually in front of the glass stream which pursues us, transforming each passing minute into a museum exhibit. Everything that we have preserved, everything that we have created remains behind us like sunken ships which remain on the sea-bed, like dead towns under a thick layer of congealed transparent lava. We are rushing forward, the River slips silently behind our backs, and years are left behind like old photographs on a desk pressed down by the Glass of Time. So our monument is just a very long plate of glass resting on 2001 columns.

Page 42
A. Brodsky, I. Utkin, *The Intelligent Market*, 1987

We begin our way with a firm decision to learn and understand everything. Endless corridors with endless niches — we must observe each of them. Every next turn gives us a new perspective with new niches. And at the end of the way — the last glance at all that what we have gone through.

Page 44
A. Brodsky, I. Utkin, *A Bridge Above the Precipice in the High Mountains*, 1987

A chapel with glass walls, glass roof and glass floor standing over a fathomless endless crack, between two abysses-upper and lower.

Page 45
A. Brodsky, I. Utkin, *Electronic Dungeon*, 1987

If I were Japanese and had a family I would build myself a little white fortress with very thick walls. I would fill these walls with everything necessary for life, with all electronic and mechanical comforts of the past, present and future. And between these walls I would create a chaos similar to that existing in my soul. A chaos of soil, wood, stones and water, a well-thought-out and a carefully protected one at that. I would make a small hole in the eastern wall to watch the sunrise and a large skylight above to light up the chaos. I would have two cars suspended like drawbridges with the help of winches. You get into the car retracted into the house. It is lowered to the ground and you drive away. And I would live with my family in this fortress enjoying the chaos in its electronic cover.

Page 47
A. Brodsky, I. Utkin, *Ship of Fools or Wooden Skyscraper for a Jolly Company*, 1988

And so, we praise you, Plague!
We fear not the darkness of the grave,
We are not perturbed by your imminent call!
We're lifting our cups of frothy wine
And inhaling the breath of the rose-like girl
Which might already be plagued!

A.S. Pushkin
A Feast During the Plague

Come join us, brothers, all ye rogues!
We've set out on a journey around the globe,

We are bound for the Land of Fools,
But, alas, we've run aground!

Sebastian Brant
The Ship of Fools (Retranslated from Russian)

Page 48/49
N. Bronzova, *Spice-and-Honey-Cake House*
Competition of the Moscow Branch of the USSR Architects' Union Building for Kropotkinskaya Street, 1984, 3rd Prize

A Spice-and-Honey-Cake House is a sample of the most delicious and healthiest architecture of which we know and dream since childhood. To build such a house take: 100 tons of wheat flour, 30 tons of sugar (salt and baking powder to taste), 7 buckets of cloves, 10 tons of honey, 5 buckets of saffron, a boxcar-load of eggs, 25 tons of water and 6 buckets of rum. Mix the ingredients, whip the mixture and bake at 500 degrees Centigrade. If the dough rises higher than recommended take the furnace apart and continue baking the cake at a lower temperature. Five to six hours later brush the cake with melted butter, sour cream and yolk. Floors, roof-beams, rafters and the staircase with balusters should be made of bitter chocolate and sweets. Windows are of lollipop and candied fruit, and the doors of chocolate waffles and cookies. Furniture is made of sweet or salty dough according to the architect's wish. The stuffing is made of cream, various kinds of jam, berries and fruit — whatever you prefer. Then everything is eaten up to the foundation and cooked again by another architect. Missing components should be bought in the neighboring bakery.

Page 50
N. Bronzova, M. Filippov, *Museum of Sculpture*, 1983
JA Competition, 2nd Prize

The home of sculpture is a garden with marble statues. A glass-sided pavilion is the place where the statues are deposited in the wintertime. Citizens are invited to create their own sculptures of snow in open spaces. When spring comes sculptures are returned to their place in the garden, while masterpieces created in winter are exhibited in the glass pavilion. Now it becomes a house of ice amid the warmth and rich foliage of summer.

Page 51
N. Bronzova, M. Filippov, *Noah's Ark*, 1987
JA Competition, Glass Monument for the Year 2001, Honorable Mention

Noah's Ark is a monument to the past millennium. Through

the maze of centuries and cultural strata we see the main thing contributed by each century to our common civilisation. The Ark resembles Chinese boxes inserted into one another. Their walls depict an ideal city as seen in each of the past ten centuries. The last stratum is from the year 2001. It symbolizes a new dream − the quest for preserving the cultural heritage of many centuries.

The floating monument symbolizes the dream of salvation in the future flood. The glass part of the monument is a symbol of the human civilisation built in the paradise lost − a place where people, animals and plants live together. This grandiose and ephemeral structure was built in the name of recreating the fundamental harmony that has been lost.

Page 52
N. Bronzova, M. Filippov, *Bridge of Bridges,* 1987

The garden located on several islets connected with one another by bridges spans two banks of a wide river. This is a place for rest, a bridge which you can stroll at leisure, choosing any road you like.

Page 54
Dmitry Bush, Dmitry Podyapolsky, Alexandre Khomyakov, *The Cube of Infinity,* 1986

There is a contradiction between the urban space of today and the requirements of organizing the urban environment. The city is an unruly, chaotic and often decaying organism. At the same time the dwelling should be a strictly neutral space free from the drawbacks of urban life.

This project tackles the task of creating a dwelling in a modern city. It combines, on the one hand, the external and, on the other, the internal isolation of the dwelling. The principle of the relationship between a building and the environment ceases to be a law.

The exterior of the BLOCK is absolutely sterile and blank. It is designed as a means of protection against the city. According to the author's plan, the absence of architectural details, openings and other large elements seals off the dwelling from the unhealthy surrounding of the city and turns the dwelling into a bulwark of man's private life.

Page 56
Dmitry Bush, Alexander Khomyakov, *Glass Stonehenge,* 1986
JA Competition "A Glass Monument for the Year 2001"

A row of stones is covered with a glass plate carrying the next row, etc.

Page 57
D. Bush, D. Podyapolsky, A. Khomyakov, *Interplay*
JA Competition A Glass Tower, 1st Prize, 1984: Model 1988

There is a pure framework. Its inner side, richly carved, is reflecting in the complicated mirrored body. The reflection is the tower.

INTERPLAY
Reality-Reflection
Detail-Whole
Light-Shade
Past-Present
Clearness-Obscurity
Great-Small
Tightness-Freedom
Aspiration-Realization

Page 59
Dmitry Bush, Dmitry Podyapolsky, Alexander Khomyakov, *Mon Plaisir,* 1985
The Competition of the Arkhitektura SSSR Journal Second Dwelling for the City Man, 1st Prize

Even a brief spell in the countryside affords a city dweller's soul a rest and helps him recover from strains and stresses of urban life. This method of psychotherapy is underscored by the notion of catharsis. Watching a peaceful landscape, a man finds relief, recuperates from fatigue and takes delight in this 'harmless joy'.

Page 60
I. Galimov, *Temple-City,* 1988

But clocks tick on, and seasons come and go,
The names of cities change, events retain
No witnesses, and memories and tears
May not be shared... Unwanted and unsought,
The shades of loved ones shrink and slip away
And we recoil in horror from the thought
That they might reappear...

...We realize that we no longer know where lies the path
To that lone house, and run as in a dream,
Despairing, mute, to where it stood, and lo! −
Discover that the walls, the things, the colums
Are different and strange, and that we too
are strangers there...
Anna Akhmatova

A center of knowledge as the cumulative culture of the human race, of international contacts and cooperation, an architectural monument to the 2000th anniversary of mankind: this is the main idea of the project called Unity of Nations Palace. Erected in all the countries willing to participate in the project, these structures will reflect each nation's measure of understanding of mankind's past, present and future. A network of such structures will symbolize social and technical progress of our planet more fully and in a more democratic way than any single architectural monument whose location might be disputed.

Located in different countries the palaces will be connected by invisible threads of telecommunication "bridges". Technical problems of telecommunications via space satellites have been practically solved. But the 21st centrury has to realize the social and psychological consequences of new forms of human communication and to implement them in architecture.

Telecommunications not only transmit information to faraway countries but also affords live communication of large numbers of people in front of huge television screens. The effect of joint participation is enormously increased due to the involvement of the population of the entire planet. The humanity thus gets a unique opportunity of seeing itself in a "television mirror". Every human being will be able to realize that he is a citizen of the world, an inhabitant of our common home, a passenger in a spaceship named the Earth. This should create a feeling of personal responsibility for safeguarding peace in the world and of the need to act in the interests of a peaceful future of mankind.

Unity of Nations Palace is to become a world-wide theater, a telespace terminal. Its chief element is a system of videoscreens and a videostage specially equipped for human communication during direct telecasts via space satellites.

Being the central information and cultural center of a country, the terminal unites a variety of structures serving different purposes, such work and exhibition premises, storage rooms, information services, lecture halls, and so forth.

The terminal is to become an embodiment of human communication in its most democratic and technically advanced form. It should stimulate creative and social activity of the people. The architectural image of the complex of structures should be able to produce a strong and lingering visual impression. It should be regarded as a universal architectural symbol by which our age might hope to be judged by posterity.

Modern architecture lacks a democratic and socially important structure of this kind, a structure would express the spirit of our age in a measure comparable to old Greek and Roman temples and forums, or Medieval Gothic cathedrals and market squares. The casual juxtaposition of edifices of various heights and shapes and the absence of a single dominant structure organizing the surrounding areas make our modern cities look chaotically monotonous.

Accumulating the highest achievements of civilisation-science, technology and art-the terminal is to become a sanctuary of the coming age, a temple of the public movement with which mankind's hopes for peace, world unity and further economic and cultural progress are associated. Being a center for human communication, a window on the world, a school for cooperation, the terminal will introduce a new organizing element into the spatial structure and the silhouette of the cities of tomorrow.

Staying in his second dwelling — a cottage in the countryside — an urban dweller will be filled with get new spatial impressions if the second dwelling resembles anything but his city apartment. Flowers, plates of fruit and favorite articles. In this case even dull cottages will look like still lifes.

It's time we took care of the Earth's silhouette. For it should look as trendy as that of Halley's Comet or that of Saturn. For that purpose it is quite enough to create a third hemisphere, a flat one. It will tackle a lot of problems, such as the shortage of raw materials, ecology, energy, transportation — you name it. What is more, it will make it possible to see an inclined horizon — the eighth wonder of the world. It does not matter that we will have to change the contours of continents, displace oceans and cope with the lower crust of the Earth, for this is only a supposition, an effort to peek into the atelier of an architect living circa 3000.

The idea of the proposed design was prompted by an "attraction" of sorts in the form of an esplanade and a "romantic" arbour. The plane of the esplanade located 13 to 14 meters above the street level affords a good panoramic view.

The second element of the structure is a small multi-functional hall for theater shows, concerts, and so forth. This hall, in the opinion of the authors, will make the place more attractive.

The portal of the theater fills in the gap between the neighboring buildings in Kropotkinskaya Street. The main divisions of the facade accord with the neighboring buildings. The inclined roof is a grass-covered slope laid out as a properly landscaped park.

Page 66
A. Krupin, A. Miroshin, V. Tregubova, *The Intelligent Market*
JA Competition, 1987, Honorable Mention

The market always was a space where exchange took place. Exchange to goods; goods to money, etc.. The intelligent market must decide functions of sale, purchase and exchange of minds. Interior space for acceptance, storage and processing of the ideas, exterior for the exposition.

Page 67
Totan Kuzembayev, Andrei Ivanov, Vyacheslav Aristov, *Bulwark of Resistance*, 1985
JA Competition Bulwark of Resistance, 1st Prize

One of the tasks of architecture from time immemorial was to protect human life. Standing up against the elements, enemies and evil spirits, man worked out archetypes of resistance. Enclosed living space is the basis of the sense of psychological protection. A fence, a fortress wall, an atrium, a city block and a square covered on four sides, a magic circle are examples of closed space. The transition from open space to enclosed space is always a multi-stage process. First you go through the city gate, walk down the street or alley, enter the gateway, go through the door, cross the anteroom. It is only then that you find yourself in a dwelling. It can be likened to a multi-layer filter. Finally, a protected microcosm comes to resemble the macrocosm in complexity, diversity and the multitude of vital elements. A palace in Split, a Russian monastery and a Japanese village are models of a universe with its symbolic and functional centers, systems of landmarks, busy and quiet places, and its own nature, both virgin and transformed.

However, with time it was becoming more and more difficult to create an organic surrounding. Designs of ideal cities from the Renaissance epoch already bore signs of imminent danger. Cohesive, yet fragile, cultural systems collapsed on impact with technology, and people became estranged from the world and from one another.

The chaos of present-day cities provokes chaos in man's inner life. A person suffering from solitude and lack of understanding, unprotected either spatially or spiritually, hovers between good and evil, seeking order and purity.

It is essential to single out fundamental elements of existence, measure their value by aggravating contradictions between them to the limit, and bring them together in a new combination.

The energy of passions, human activity, everyday fuss and self-destruction is allowed to make its way into the Bulwark. But the colonnade purifies and transforms it, as if reading this energy for going into the yards-the world of contemplation, purification and self-knowledge.

A forest of columns turns into a living forest, the multitude of chaotic thoughts blends into one clear idea.

Protecting nature we are protecting our own existence. Trying to cognize nature and perceive its essence, we seek and find our own ego.

The Bulwark of Purity — purity of soil, water, air and thoughts — is a symbol of a new, better organized and more meaningful life.

Page 69
T. Kuzembayev, I. Pishchukevich, *Dwelling for Tomorrow*, 1987
The competition of the Arkhitektura SSSR Journal, 3rd Prize

In this age of technology man is increasingly striving to individualize his surrounding and restore his contact with nature. This is an instance of subconscious resistance to the undivided reign of machines which oust human spirit from our life: what suits machines perfectly will far from always satisfy man. In this project we endeavored to combine technical progress with the interests of the individual and find a way for a harmonious coexistence of both.

The proposed living unit is a big cube having an inner yard with smaller cubes, or one-family "homes" (modul 1), placed inside. The latter can be filled in their turn with 27 cubes measuring 3 by 3 meters, primary elements of the dwelling (module 2).

Module 1 is a place where the family meets, a versatile space which can perform, depending on what it is filled with, any functions in line with the family needs.

Module 2 is a place of seclusion for meeting one's individual needs. It can be isolated completely, or, on the contrary, opened partially or completely. Individual modules are used for sleeping, watching movies, going in for sports, and communicating with nature (large aquariums, sections of a forest or a desert). Everything is based on the contrast and interaction between supertechnology and nature (plants, sand, water, fire), new and traditional materials (bricks, lumber, stone, etc.), and the simultaneous presence of the future and the past.

Modules (No. 2) will be turned out by manufacturing plants and bought at stores the way we now buy furniture. A new resident of the unit will replace old modules, thus creating a new house in line with his tastes and outlook on the world. Everyone will be able to build a house for himself. Using modules (No. 2), one can create both traditional and avant-garde interiors, go back to nature or find oneself in the center of a modern city. Industrially-built dwellings of that type will be in high demand in the future, meeting diverse individual requirements. For they will be free from the main short-coming of the present-day dwelling, its conservatism, and will not grow morally obsolete before getting old physically.

Page 71
Y. Kuzin, Shanghai 1987, *Japan House for Today Competition*

A heavy, blanketing fog separates the world into the visible and invisible parts. In much the same manner lives this city, where the secret and personal get mixed with the common and communal.

Page 72
Y. Kuzin, *City Sockets*, 1988
IAA and IFYA Competition Space for a 21st-Century Civilization, 1st Prize

Who are they?
The Computer – a red box that remembers everything.
The Coordinator – an airship that gives directions and carries things.
The Informer – a tower that screens things and communicates with others of the same kind.
The Transformer – a mechanism providing everyone with fuel.
The Queer – a hollow metal giant without any functions.

The Chronicle:
Five metallic guys set off on a long journey.
One gave directions to all others.
Another thought of all others.
Yet another carried fuel for all.
The fourth could speak.
And the fifth simply joined others.

Page 73
M. Labazov, A. Cheltsov, *Dwelling as a Reflection of Self*
King Fahd Award Competition, 1986, 1st Prize

The intent of this project was to arrive at a flexible system of architectural and spatial forms reflecting the importance of economic, cultural, religious and functional factors. We relied on the laws governing the spatial structure of a Moslem home, block and city and proceeded from the traditions of reinforced tower-like dwellings found in Yemen. The smallest element in the hierarchy of architectural spaces – the inner hall, the guest and communal zones which form the main image of the home – is isolated into an inner one-and-a-half or double-height unit reflecting personal tastes of the owner. The hall is crowned with a mihrab (placed freely inside the house, it indicates the direction of Mecca). This small unit – a family temple – is located within the house proper which depends on the tastes and interests of the family. A large building/tower which comprises the living space complete with an inner hall, guest and ancillary yards is surrounded by a semi-transparent cover and demonstrates the interests of the block and of society where it is located. The cover consists of light-weight timber, plastic or metal structures, or of glass, and may serve as a greenhouse and as a panel of solar batteries. It can reproduce any ornament, concealing the European or Moslem image of the building, the wealth or poverty of the family, its tastes and interests, and enables the house to exist in an alien cutural context, expressing the idea of social brotherhood characteristic of Moslem society. Space between the coating and the building is reserved for its future development. Time flies and man's tastes change, the family grows, the mores of society change too, and the house may change with them: the communal image of the home (the cover) changes easily, living space is expanded or re-built and the soul of the home-the hall-changes its decoration. It is possible to build the house on the basis of different principles (hall-type house/castle, house/castle with a central hall, central courtyard, etc.). The principle of closed volume without windows on the outside perimeter of the walls or with windows employing reflected light, and the 'sky well' system make diverse forms of blocking possible depending on specific requirements and surroundings. In any case, looking at the external image of the house it is impossible to determine the organization of its inner space (hall-type or open-type), because the closed volume remains unchanged in all versions.

Page 74
Mikhail Labazov, Andrei Savvin, *Genius Loci*, 1984
The Competition of the Arkhitektura SSSR Journal Problem and Decision, 3rd Prize

Each territory retains a memory of culture related to it: from the reflection of elements of a territory in folklore to their fixation in the structure of historical traditions. The main meaning of a territory as a cultural phenomenon is in giving the individual of today a chance to identify himself with the spiritual traditions of his people: in a city, village, field or forest.

Culture turns movement through actual space into motion that accords with the laws of myth and tale: a road, a boundary, a bridge, a road-fork and a center-all these are typical elements of mythological space.

A professional is striving to create a quantitative diversity of habitats, while culture is striving to preserve a qualitative diversity of mythical and poetic space. It is in the context of architectural and historical thinking that GENIUS LOCI is born.

Page 76
L. Pavlov. M. Bartenev, V. Shteller, N. Gorkin, *Personal Perception Theater*
Competition of the USSR Union of Architects Future Theater, 1978 1st Prize

1. Personal perception and reaction are not suppressed by people around
2. All spectators are at an equal distance from the stage and at the same time are as close to it as possible.
3. The scale of the show may change as action is going on (close-up, medium close-up, long distance)
4. Dead space is absent and the volume of the hall is minimized
5. The foyer/slope creates a maximum of possibilities for communication.

Page 77
Vyacheslav Petrenko, *Reflections Over the Theme,* 1981

The Marc Square, named so in honor of Marc Chagall, an artist who portrayed people floating in the air. As a rule horizontal planes of human activity are separated from one another, and people are bound to them by the force of gravity. However, there are moments when man is able to command the evironment-these are moments of special elation, but such moments are given to us very rarely. Usually, you have to go to some special place to experience them. Further, the horizontal plane of activity is organized, at best, according to the pattern in which various objects are placed on it. But here, the horizontal plane is shaped by shadows floating on its surface. This creates the impression that moving non-material elements are present on the plane.

Page 82
L. Batalow, V. Zaitsev, *Path*
JA Competition, *Museum of Sculpture,* Honorable Mention, 1983

The Path is a Museum of Sculpture.
The Path traversed by the Creator from the source of talent to the Ocean of Genius
The Path of a collector is from an accidental find to a meaningful search.
The Path of the visitor is to cognition.
It embodies a complex and contradictory artistic personality. Different volumes that are gradually lost in the environment, varying heights, diverse degrees of lighting and a change in the direction of motion along the "stream". Only they can convey the meaning of constraint, self-confidence, doubt, crises and discorveries.
Combinations of spaces can be viewed, regardless of the exposition, as stages of the artistic Path.
Having sensed what volume is all about and walking from a lonely statue through the halls, the visitor stops at the last statue, turns back and realizes that he had traversed a difficult and great Path.

Page 83
V. Zaitsev, L. Batalov, *Rising to the Peak*
JA Competition, Glass Monument for the Year 2001, Honorable Mention, 1986

The year 2001 is yet another peak conquered by mankind
The glass monument for the year 2001 commemorates Mankind's striving to rise to the Peak.
Files of people engraved on glass climb to the top and descend to the foot of the monument in the hope to reach the Peak guarded by impenetrable glass.
Everyone who approaches the monument joins in that perpetual movement up and down the transparent stairs.
People who are climbing the stairs resemble pilgrims walking along a tortuous road in the hope to touch a far-away star.
Why are they striving to reach the Peak?
What will he who has risen to the Peak gain?

Page 85
I. Shalmin, *Single-Pier Bridge,* 1987

Instability of our relations yields its place to stable contacts only if we move toward each other.

Page 87
D. Shelest, A. Shelest, *Cross-Country Cottage, City Man's*

l Second Dwelling,
Competition Sponsored by the Arkhitektura SSSR Journal, 1985, 1st Prize

1. In your absence or in wintertime the cottage is placed on its foundation in the middle of a tiny land plot (where your garden is situated) and connected to service lines.
2. The cottage is easily propelled with the help of a hand-driven mechanism and can travel through the settlement at a speed of 5 kpm.
3. Ascending a bank.
4. Check weighing and the issue of pontoons and air balloons.
5. The cottage takes only 10 minutes to launch!
6. The cottage takes off from water or from a ground pad. Watch the cottage travel upstream and return downstream!
WARNING. Do not try to take the drive apart, never uncork the pontoon and do not buy our competitors' products.

Page 88
A. Sigachev, *21st-Century Space,* 1988
IAA and IFYA Competition, 1988 Honorable Mention

Cities will remain the same in the 21st century. Much time will pass before they turn into ingots of metal and glass. But for now the city is an organism suffering from the disease of over-saturation, over-population, over-pollution and over-concentration.
Spaces for recreation and amusement developing on a purely emotional basis (like abstract art), if introduced into the present-day city, can save it from the disease of over-saturation.
The result will show itself in the late 21st century.

Page 91
A. Cheltsov, M. Labazov, *Aquarium City,* 1987

"Why did you pull me out of the sea?"
Rafael Alberti

Fig. 1. Buildings around the body of water.
Fig. 2. "A place by the ocean, in candlelight;

Surrounded by a field overgrown with clover, sorrel and alfalfa...
Falling into the grass, the owl catches the mouse,
Roof-beams creak for no obvious reason.
You sleep better in a wooden city,
'cause you dream only what actually happened.
It smells of fresh fish, the profile of a chair got stuck to the wall, thin gauze is lazily stirring in the window and is adjusted by the tide's beam Like a falling quilt."
I. Brodsky

Fig. 3. Future city
3A. The Past
3B. The Present
3C. The Future
Fig 4. Future city in the Sea
Swimming in the ocean,
Flying through the ocean
Blue water
Blue water is around
And the sea stars
Ant the lobsters
Are swimming toward
Are flying toward
YOU...
A. Vovk
4B. Venice

Page 92
Sergei Chuklov, Vera Chuklova, *Age of Glass,* 1986
JA Competition A Glass Monument for the Year 2001, Honorable Mention

AGE OF GLASS
THE MONUMENT...
...for the Year 2001 is a Glass Square through the paving of which you can see Squares of the Gold/Silver/Bronze/and Iron Ages

Page 93
Sergei Chuklov, Vera Chuklova, *Edge-Junction-Limit-Boundary,* 1987

... Between the surfaces of the detail
between two materials,
the wall and the air,
this minute is clamped, as if
between the PAST and the FUTURE.

Page 95
S. Chuklov, V. Chuklova, *A Stone Cast into the Water,* 1988

While deeper penetrating nature, we leave behind ourselves a geometrical landscape. 21st century: a stone cast into the water makes squares.

Page 96
D. Velichkin, V. Levi, D. Shelest, *Camera-Museum*
JA Competition Museum of Sculpture, 1983 2nd Prize

The museum is situated in one of the streets of the city besides an endless row of dull and monotonous buildings.

Like the nymph Daphne who chose to become a laurel rather than lose her freedom, the sculpture is striving to go beyond the bounds of the limited space toward natural light and freedom.

A person in the focus of the camera can see an illusory image of the sculpture emerging in the hole in one of the museum's walls – a hole which serves simultaneously as a window on nature.

The impression from the illusory image makes one go further-beyond somber-looking city streets and into the domain of freedom and light.

Page 97
D. Velichkin, A. Bel'ayev, V. Levi, *Red Tower,* 1986
International Competition Dwelling for Today, Honorable Mention

"My home is my castle."

All service functions are concentrated inside the building within a unit measuring 3x3x3 meters: a kitchen, a toilet room, a bathroom, a heating system and a staircase placed at an angle of 45 degrees and leading to the second level of the unit, where the parents' bedroom is located. Each side of the tower/unit has two partitions that can be moved in the unoccupied space of the building. The partitions bear the imprint of the function which they are called upon to conceal, and only their frontals serve as decorative elements. When the partitions are retracted eight accommodations are formed sufficient for a family of five (parents and three children). When the partitions are in place a family of two lives inside the tower surrounded by the 'castle' of unoccupied space.

Page 98
V. Voronova, A. Ignatyev, A. Petrov, *Center for Leisure-Time Activities and Communication*
Competition of the Arkhitektura SSSR Journal, 1984

The main architectural and planning idea of the Center is as follows: it is a system of open and roofed courtyards with premises of similar functions located around. The intent was to achieve a surprise effect by contrasting narrow corridors and light-filled courts of various shapes. Each of the latter contains an element denoting the function of the premises, for instance, a fir-tree, a fountain, a statue, a pavilion, and so forth. We were after an architectural environment corresponding to man's needs-a "humanized" architectural environment, where people, not architecture or empty space, will play the leading role.

Page 99
V. Voronova, A. Ignatyev, A. Petrov, *One-Day Atrium*
JA Competition Space with an Atrium, 1985, 2nd Prize

Every town has its own Carnival, a day in the year when citizens sing, dance and enjoy themselves. The Carnival takes place right on the streets; it has no specific space. Lets turn the streets into an Enfilade of Atria formed by vertical and horizontal pieces of colored canvas. This would be a real Carnival space-changeable and joyful.